THE POCKET
SCOTTISH MOVIE BOOK

BRIAN PENDREIGH

MAINSTREAM
PUBLISHING

EDINBURGH AND LONDON

For Mum and Dad
and the memory of all those
nights at the pictures in North Berwick

First published in Great Britain in 2002 by
MAINSTREAM PUBLISHING COMPANY (EDINBURGH) LTD
7 Albany Street
Edinburgh EH1 3UG

ISBN 1 84018 648 8

Published in association with Scottish Screen, VisitScotland, the British Council
and the Scottish Highlands and Islands Film Commission in celebration
of the Film Industry in Scotland

A catalogue record for this book is available from the British Library

Typeset in Helvetica and Van Dijck
Printed and bound in Great Britain by
The Bath Press

FOREWORD

It was the late 1960s and I was a schoolboy in Edinburgh when one Saturday morning my father took me to see a film being made not far from where we lived in Comely Bank. Someone told me one of the girls in my class was in it, but I didn't see her among the throng of schoolgirls dodging between the oddly old-fashioned cars with their running boards. This was the Swinging '60s, like I said. But the film was from another era – it was *The Prime of Miss Jean Brodie*. I waited an eternity for it to appear in the cinemas, and when it did it was an X certificate and I had to go on waiting.

In due course I would visit many more film sets and would even visit *Jean Brodie*'s director Ronald Neame at his home in Los Angeles when I went to the Oscars the year *Braveheart* won. *Trainspotting* had opened the previous month and had been hailed the best British film of the decade.

They seem like bookends now – that first schoolboy set visit to *Jean Brodie* at one end, and *Braveheart* and *Trainspotting* at the other. How do you top the best picture Oscar? But maybe they are not so much bookends, as chapters. After the Oscar there would be new chapters. Ewan McGregor went on to play Obi-Wan Kenobi; Ewen Bremner reinvented himself as an action hero in *Pearl Harbor* and *Black Hawk Down*; suddenly Scottish actors were everywhere – Ray Park as Darth Maul, Billy Boyd as Pippin in *The Lord of the Rings* and Robbie Coltrane as Hagrid in the *Harry Potter* films.

There was a time when a film, any film, that was shooting in Scotland constituted a big news story. Not any more. With hits on the screen and the new Scottish Screen agency to offer advice and lottery funding, Scotland is a hive of film-making. Lars von Trier came here to make *Breaking the Waves* and I took my own children to watch *Jude* shooting in Edinburgh's High Street. There were some disappointments. There was a lot more buzz about Robert Duvall's football film *A Shot at Glory* and *Women Talking Dirty*, the first film from Elton John's production company, when they were shooting than when they eventually opened. But, as we go to press in 2002, there are high hopes for *Young Adam*, Ewan McGregor's first feature in Scotland since *Trainspotting*, for *Morvern Callar* and for *The Rocket Post*, a fascinating story of romance and scientific eccentricity in the Outer Hebrides.

By the time of *Braveheart* and *Trainspotting*, I had been writing about film in Scotland for a decade. I was a professional film journalist, but I was also still a fan. It is not only the big stars who interest, charm and occasionally disappoint me; it is the stories behind the films, tracking down the locations that were used, exploring the highways and byways of cinema's present and its past, and, of course, predicting its future course. As a boy, I worshipped Kirk Douglas. I would stick my finger in my chin and press the flesh to try to produce a cleft like his. I got to meet him in Palm Springs a few years ago, though I would have liked to have been there when he came to Scotland to make *Catch Me a Spy*, back in the 1970s, a modest little entry in this book. I have *Jean Brodie* on video now and I replayed it while writing this book in an attempt to confirm exactly where it was in Edinburgh that she stayed – not far from Sean Connery as it turns out, not far geographically, but a long way socially. And while writing that entry I got sidetracked onto the St Trinian's films and their Edinburgh roots.

This book is for industry insiders, fans and tourists. It is for anyone who has ever enjoyed a film set in Scotland or featuring Scottish actors, and when the end-credits rolled has been left wanting to know a little more. It covers the films, the locations, the stars and the interesting little byways of Scottish cinema.

And I never did spot that former classmate in *The Prime of Miss Jean Brodie*. She may even not have been in it. It doesn't matter, she was just a MacGuffin anyway. MacGuffin – you'll find the entry between Ewan McGregor and Kevin McKidd.

IAN BANNEN

At a time when few feature films shot in Scotland, Ian Bannen was the only Scottish actor regularly landing major roles in international movies, other than Sean

Connery, with whom he shared the same theatre stage, house and even girlfriend at various times. They made two under-rated films together, *The Hill* (1965), set in a tough military detention camp, and *The Offence* (1972), a harrowing drama in which Bannen's suspected child molester provokes Connery's police officer into beating him to death. Bannen was born in Airdrie, though the family home was in neighbouring Coatbridge where his father was a lawyer. Bannen's acting career spanned more than half a century and his roles included Hamlet for the Royal Shakespeare Company; the betrayed spy who kills the mole in the celebrated television drama series *Tinker, Tailor, Soldier, Spy*; Dr Cameron in the revival of the *Doctor Finlay* series; and Robert the Bruce's leprous father in *Braveheart*. He could be either avuncular or quietly chilling. More often he was the supporting

Ian Bannen (Scottish Screen)

player rather than the star, but one of his greatest triumphs came at the end of his career with the success in 1999 of the comedy *Waking Ned*, in which he had a lead role as one of two elderly schemers with their sights set on the lottery winnings of a dead friend. The part reflected some of his real-life roguish charm. Bannen had just started work on the Scottish film *Strictly Sinatra* when he was killed in a car crash.

BRIGITTE BARDOT

Brigitte Bardot is not the first name that comes to mind when considering Scottish films, but the legendary French sex kitten caused a stir when she turned up to shoot her latest helping of steamy Gallic naughtiness, *A Cœur Joie*, in East Lothian at the height of the Swinging '60s. The story of a French model embarking on an ill-advised affair with a younger man may have been typical Bardot, but the location was not. Director Serge Bourguignon, who had recently won an Oscar for *Sundays and Cybele*, wanted a romantic setting. He came to Scotland, watched a short film that included shots of Dirleton Castle, 15 miles east of Edinburgh, and decided it was sufficiently picturesque and convenient. He then confirmed his choice on the basis of the quality of the food at the Open Arms Hotel. The film was released in Britain under the title *Two Weeks in September* but disappeared without trace.

BOLLYWOOD

Hollywood film producers are not the only ones who have been drawn by Scotland's dramatic scenery and historic buildings in recent years. Their counterparts from Bollywood have been coming in increasing numbers, following the success of *Kuch Kuch Hota Hai* (*Something is Happening*) in the late 1990s. At £1.5 million, it was a big-budget film by Indian standards, with locations in India, Mauritius and Scotland, but it grossed that in the UK alone and opened the floodgates for other Indian film-makers. Scottish Screen makes the official count fifteen in five years, but some producers have preferred to make arrangements through uncles or cousins resident in Scotland, rather than through the national film agency. The economics and practicalities of Bollywood film-making are very different from those in Hollywood. *Kuch Kuch*'s crew stayed at Glasgow University's halls of residence and did their own cooking, while another crew brought traffic to a halt with an unauthorised song-and-dance number in the middle of Glasgow's Sauchiehall Street. 'Normally you scout the land and check permissions,' noted Scottish Screen's location manager, Kevin Cowle. 'With Bollywood crews, you'd be driving along the shores of a loch and they would say, "That looks nice, let's stop here."'

The US produces about 350 features a year, India twice as many. The word Bollywood is an amalgamation of Hollywood and Bombay, although Madras is also a major production centre. It has been applied to popular Indian cinema that mixes action, drama, romance and sudden bursts of song and dance. Traditionally, Bollywood film-makers went to Kashmir for dramatic mountain backdrops, but were encouraged to look elsewhere by political unrest there. Switzerland was an early beneficiary and London also proved popular for its familiar landmark buildings. In 1996 *Main Solah Baras Ki* (*I Am Sweet Sixteen*) combined these with Scottish locations, including Edinburgh Castle, the Forth and Tay Bridges, Loch Lomond, Glen Coe and Glen Nevis, Stirling Castle, Urquhart Castle on Loch Ness, Aviemore and Aberdeen city centre and airport. As well as spectacular scenery and historic buildings, Bollywood producers have also regarded shopping malls and modern universities as signs of sophistication and affluence, and *Main Solah Baras Ki* was shot on the rooftop plaza of Edinburgh's Princes Mall.

Kuch Kuch turned a novelty into a fashion. Scottish locations included Eilean Donan Castle; Tantallon Castle, near North Berwick; Crossraguel Abbey in Ayrshire; Ross Priory at Loch Lomond; Inchmahome Priory near Aberfoyle; and Black Rock Cottage in Glen Coe, although the film was not set in Scotland. Bollywood films have a habit simply of tossing foreign locations into scenes, particularly the staple song-and-dance numbers, without any explanation. Three hours long, with Hindi dialogue, *Kuch Kuch* made the British Top Ten. *Pyaar Ishq aur Mohabbat (Love, Love and Love)* (2001), another big Bollywood production, was the story of an Indian girl at Glasgow University. Numerous locations in Glasgow included the university, George Square, the Clyde Tunnel, Springfield Quay and even the Scottish Screen offices in West George Street. It also shot in and around Edinburgh city centre, at Stirling Castle, Paisley Abbey and Crossraguel Abbey, Bearsden, Ayr, Loch Lomond, Rosyth, Dumbarton, Clyde football club's ground at Cumbernauld, Prestwick Airport and Culzean Castle in Ayrshire, which had also served as the seat of Lord Summerisle in *The Wicker Man*.

BILLY BOYD

As a bookbinder at Collins print works in Bishopbriggs, near Glasgow, one of Billy Boyd's jobs was putting the covers on *The Lord of the Rings*. He never read it at the time, but years later he would help to bring Tolkien's trilogy to life for cinema audiences all over the world as the hobbit Pippin. Coming from a

working-class Glasgow family, acting was not an obvious career option and it was only after completing his apprenticeship that he considered drama school. Boyd worked extensively in theatre, but had no significant film roles before *The Lord of the Rings*. At 5 ft 6 in., he was the right height, and his sharp youthful features seemed well-suited for Pippin, the young hobbit whose impetuous behaviour often lands the heroes in trouble, and director Peter Jackson was impressed by his idea of playing Pippin with a Scottish accent. At 33, Boyd suddenly found himself to be an international film star.

Billy Boyd (Brunskill Management)

BRAVEHEART (1995)

The story of the Oscar-winning film *Braveheart* did not begin with Hollywood superstar Mel Gibson, but with an American tourist and a visit to Edinburgh Castle. Randall Wallace was a struggling novelist when he visited Scotland on holiday in 1983. At the entrance to the castle he was met by two great stone warriors and, although the names of Robert the Bruce and William Wallace have been revered by generations of Scots, they meant nothing to Randall. Although Bruce has been the more celebrated figure, having secured Scottish independence at the Battle of Bannockburn in 1314. Randall was more taken with his namesake, William Wallace, the son of a small landowner who had previously led the Scots to victory against the English at Stirling Bridge. Although he was ultimately defeated and executed, his example laid the foundations for Bruce's triumph a few years later.

Mel Gibson in *Braveheart* (20th Century Fox)

Randall Wallace considered it 'the greatest adventure story in history' and thought it could make an epic historical novel. The only problem was that he was already writing an epic historical novel, set in Russia. It would occupy four years of his life and fail to find a publisher. By then Randall was working in television, so he decided to attempt to turn William Wallace's story into a film script. Wallace lived on the edge of the Dark Ages and historical details are sketchy. However, there are references to the killing of his wife, so Randall let his imagination fly, with a story of a reluctant hero seeking vengeance for the murder of a loved one.

The screenplay was completed in 1992 and two years later was in production. The town of Lanark lies south-east of Glasgow in the Central Belt, but in Hollywood movies Scotland has always been a place of romantic misty mountains and heathery glens, so Lanark was rebuilt in Glen Nevis, in the shadow of Britain's highest peak Ben Nevis, near where *Rob Roy* would shoot a few weeks later. The earth-roofed plaster houses and thriving marketplace were removed after filming, though the *Braveheart* car park, constructed to service the film, remained. The announcement that some of the shooting would be done in Ireland prompted an outcry in the press. Much was made of Irish tax incentives and the availability of soldiers as extras, though Mel Gibson, who was director and producer as well as star, told me that a key factor was the availability of horses for battle scenes. There was also some shooting at Glen Coe and in the Kinlochleven area.

Braveheart was a stunning epic reminiscent of *El Cid* and *Ben-Hur*, with brilliant battle scenes and stirring dialogue. It went on to win five Oscars, including best picture, and Scotland benefited from unprecedented worldwide exposure. A survey in 1996, the year after *Braveheart* was released, showed cinema had been a factor in the choice of Scotland as a holiday destination for a fifth of American visitors. Visitor figures more than doubled at the Wallace Monument at Stirling, an impressive tower that affords superb views across the countryside where the battle for Scotland's destiny was fought.

Braveheart prompted a Government review of film-making in Scotland and the establishment of the Scottish Screen agency. It also had a huge effect on popular culture: in its opening month it was mentioned in 74 articles in *The Scotsman*, football supporters adopted the blue war paint Gibson sported in the movie, political commentators started talking about 'the *Braveheart* factor' and support for the Scottish National Party soared. Within a few years Scots had voted for their own parliament, restoring a measure of the independence for which Wallace and Bruce had fought.

BREAKING THE WAVES (1996)

Many viewers hailed it as a modern classic. Others were disgusted by it, some quite literally, with viewers throwing up in the cinema. Rarely has a film divided audiences quite as much as Lars von Trier's melodrama about a fey young woman from a remote community, seemingly on the west coast of Scotland, and her ill-fated marriage to a foreign oil-rig worker. The culture clash is summed up brilliantly in the wordless scene at the wedding reception where an oil-rig worker downs a can of Younger's Tartan Special in one gulp and a grey-bearded elder responds by draining a half-pint of what looks like barley water; the oil-rig worker crushes the can, with a smile, and the elder responds by crushing his glass, without a hint of humour. The film captures the oppressiveness of an introspective and strict presbyterian society – even though the film was not originally set in Scotland. It was written and directed by a Dane, and von Trier planned to shoot in Jutland, then Norway, Belgium and Ireland before settling on Scotland (though he also shot in a Danish studio and on location there).

Emily Watson won an Oscar nomination for her performance as the child-like Bess, who talks directly to God. Distraught when her new husband (Stellan Skarsgard) returns to work, she begs God to return him to her. Her prayer is answered at a cost – Jan is paralysed in a workplace accident.

Von Trier went on to initiate the Dogme back-to-basics movement, elements of which can be seen in the film's grainy texture and jerky hand-held camera. After two viewers were sick in the foyer, Edinburgh's Cameo cinema put up a warning notice suggesting people susceptible to motion sickness should sit at the back. Other viewers struggled with the mix of melodrama, sex and what seems like mental retardation.

The film shot on the Isle of Skye, around Neist Point Lighthouse and on the road between Uig and Staffin. It also shot in the port of Mallaig on the mainland, where locations included the harbour, Mallaig High School and the Marine Hotel, and it revisited a couple of nearby *Local Hero* locations – the Morar coastline and the disused church at Polnish. While Bill Forsyth wrong-footed viewers with a young black minister, von Trier seems to have drawn his kirk elders from a painting of two centuries earlier. Ironically, the church at Polnish, Our Lady of the Braes, was a Roman Catholic one.

EWEN BREMNER

Ewen Bremner is a national treasure. Spud's drug-fuelled job interview in *Trainspotting* was one of the most surreally funny scenes since the heyday of Monty Python. The sequence in which he and his girlfriend's mum play tug-of-war with his soiled bed-sheets, while the family sit down to breakfast, was the perfect example of gross-out comedy before the genre was invented. But the actor, once described as 'plug-ugly' by *The Sun*, seemed to disappear after that, playing junkies and losers in films that no one saw. Bremner took a year out to play music, and then went off and worked in an institution for the criminally insane in New York to prepare for a role as a schizophrenic in *Julien Donkey-Boy*. It was a great performance, but another film that no one saw. The son of two teachers, Bremner grew up in the Edinburgh seaside suburb of Portobello, attended Edinburgh Theatre Workshop, had an agent at 12 and landed a leading role, as a schoolboy, in the 1986 comedy *Heavenly Pursuits* with Tom Conti and Helen Mirren. However, he seemed destined to become the *Trainspotting* equivalent of *The Magnificent Seven*'s Brad Dexter. Brad who? Exactly! Then, suddenly, Bremner reappeared in his most unexpected and most perverse role of all – American action hero; stepping forward, alongside Ben Affleck and Josh Hartnett, as an American airman in *Pearl Harbor*, and while Affleck and Hartnett share the affections of nurse Kate Beckinsale, Bremner gets a romance all to himself. *Pearl Harbor* producer Jerry Bruckheimer was so impressed he cast him as one of the American soldiers fighting hostile African natives in the urban war movie *Black Hawk Down* – an ordinary man caught up in extraordinary circumstances. It served as an unlikely reunion with *Trainspotting* co-star Ewan McGregor and provided Spud with some decent employment at last.

BRIGADOON (1954)

Not a single frame of the 1954 Gene Kelly musical was shot in Scotland. However, it is not as if producer Arthur Freed did not consider coming to Scotland to film his story about a Scottish village that emerges from the mists for just one day in every hundred years. He toured some of Scotland's most picturesque towns and villages, including Culross, Dunkeld, Comrie (whose humpback stone bridge has long been a favourite with painters), Braemar, Inveraray and even Brig o' Doon itself. Finally, Freed was forced to conclude there was nowhere in Scotland quite Scottish enough for Brigadoon. He went home to Hollywood, built the village in the studio and filled it with Americans in tartan. For decades *Brigadoon* has been anathema to those who would rather glory in the authentic misery of *My Childhood*, but the film probably did more to promote the notion of Scotland as a land of wistful fantasy and romance than any other. And there are worse images Scotland could have had.

ROBERT CARLYLE

As a small boy, Robert Carlyle loved to go to the pictures with his dad to see the James Bond films. Sean Connery was his hero, one of the few actors who spoke like him – well, almost, since Connery was from Edinburgh, Carlyle from Glasgow. When he left school at 16, Carlyle had no thoughts of emulating Connery or appearing in a James Bond movie. Instead he followed his father's example and trained as a painter. Carlyle's mother deserted them when Carlyle was just four, leaving his father to bring him up as best he could. They moved around Britain in search of work and, from the age of seven or eight, the youngster worked on building sites with his father, scraping paint from windows, for his own little wage packet. He got book tokens for his 21st birthday, bought a copy of *The Crucible* just to make up the amount of the tokens and enjoyed it so much he started drama classes. That decision led him to the Royal Scottish Academy of Music and Drama. He worked with various

Robert Carlyle (photograph by Alan Wylie)

theatre groups after college, but it was an advert for actors with experience in the construction industry that led to his first big film break in 1990.

Ken Loach, director of the celebrated *Kes* and a leading figure in the English social-realist cinema of the 1960s, was looking for actors for *Riff-Raff*, a black comedy celebrating the spirit of casual labourers on London's building sites and exposing the dangerous conditions in which they worked. Carlyle landed the lead role of Stevie, a soft-spoken Glaswegian whose ambition is to sell boxer shorts from his own market stall. The film became an arthouse hit. He began a long association with director Antonia Bird on the BBC drama *Safe* (1993), and established a reputation as the Scottish Robert De Niro because of the lengths to which he would go to prepare for roles. For *Safe*, in which he plays a homeless person, he spent a week living and sleeping on the streets of London, begging from passers-by and rummaging through bins outside McDonald's for scraps.

Carlyle can be as gentle as a lamb or as deadly as a shark. He was chilling as Albie, the quiet *Guardian*-reading killer in the TV series *Cracker*. Carlyle maintained a Scouse accent throughout the shoot, on-screen and off. Then came Francis Begbie, the loud-mouthed psycho in a Pringle sweater in *Trainspotting*. Carlyle had already turned down a role in the same team's *Shallow Grave*. He also declined the chance to appear in *Braveheart* and *Rob Roy*, has resisted the lure of

Hollywood and continues to live in Scotland with wife Anastasia, a make-up artist he met on *Cracker*. The television series *Hamish Macbeth* gave him a plum role as a dope-smoking Highland bobby, and a big international audience, but it was the surprise success of *The Full Monty*, a comedy-drama about unemployed Sheffield steel-workers who turn themselves into an unlikely striptease act, that catapulted him into cinema's major league.

He was a highwayman in *Plunkett and Macleane* and a cannibal in the dark and under-rated western *Ravenous*, a nightmare production on which the original director was sacked. Carlyle led an actors' revolt when the studio brought in a replacement whose only previous film was *Home Alone 3*, and Antonia Bird was speedily recruited. A brief early appearance as Daffy, a manic, suicidal, drug-addled backpacker, was one of the best things about *The Beach*, though it threatened to turn the rest of the film into an anti-climax, for Leonardo DiCaprio could not compete with Carlyle's passion and intensity. He delivered a powerful performance as the father in *Angela's Ashes*, the film of Frank McCourt's recollections of a poor Irish childhood in the 1930s and 1940s, where he wallows in self-pity and alcohol, as much a victim as a villain. And, of course, Carlyle got the chance to fulfil a boyhood fantasy and appear in a James Bond movie when he played Renard, a fanatical killer who feels no pain because of the bullet in his brain that is slowly killing him, in *The World is Not Enough*.

CENTRAL SCOTLAND LOCATIONS

1. Ardkinglass House: *My Life So Far*; 2. Arnhall Castle: *Monty Python and the Holy Grail*; 3. Arran: *The Governess*; 4. Auchtermuchty: *Doctor Finlay*; 5. Barnbougle Castle: *The Prime of Miss Jean Brodie*; 6. Bishopbriggs: *Late Night Shopping*; 7. Blackness Castle: *Hamlet*; 8. Bowling: *Young Adam*; 9. Bracklinn Falls: *Monty Python and the Holy Grail*; 10. Callander: *Dr Finlay's Casebook*; 11. Cockburnspath: *The Little Vampire*, *Mrs Brown*; 12. Coldingham: *The Little Vampire*, *Women Talking Dirty*; 13. Crail: *A Shot at Glory*, *The Winter Guest*; 14. Crichton Castle: *Rob Roy*; 15. Crieff: childhood home of Ewan McGregor; 16. Culross: *Kidnapped* (1971) (as Edinburgh), *The Little Vampire*; 17. Cumbernauld: *Gregory's Girl*, *Gregory's Two Girls*; 18. Dalmeny House: *The Little Vampire*; 19. Dirleton Castle: *A Cœur Joie* (*Two Weeks in September*); 20. Doune Castle: *Monty Python and the Holy Grail*; 21. Drummond Castle: *Rob Roy*; 22. Dumbarton: *A Shot at Glory* (Boghead football ground, now housing); 23. Dunblane: *The 39 Steps* (1959); 24. Dundas Castle: *The Little Vampire*; 25. Duns Castle: *Mrs Brown*; 26. Elie: *The Winter Guest*; 27. Floors Castle: *Greystoke – The Legend of Tarzan, Lord of the Apes*; 28. Forth Bridge: *The 39 Steps* (1935), *The 39 Steps* (1959); 29. Forth Road Bridge: *Complicity*; 30. Forth and Clyde Canal:

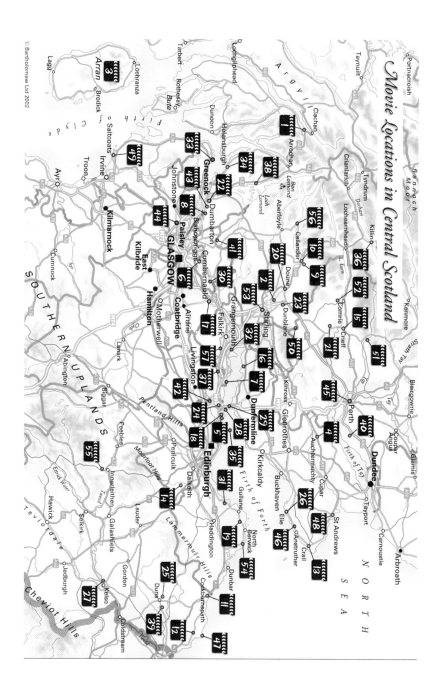

Movie Locations in Central Scotland

Young Adam; 31. Gosford House: *The House of Mirth*, *The Little Vampire*; 32. Grangemouth: *Young Adam*; 33. Greenock: *Sweet Sixteen*; 34. Helensburgh: childhood home of Deborah Kerr and Jack Buchanan; 35. Inchmickery: *Complicity*; 36. Killin: *Casino Royale*, *Monty Python and the Holy Grail*, *The 39 Steps* (1959); 37. Linlithgow: *Young Adam*; 38. Loch Lomond: *Carla's Song*, *High Road* (formerly *Take the High Road*) with the village of Luss as principal location, *Kuch Kuch Hota Hai*; 39. Manderston House: *The House of Mirth*, *Mrs Brown*; 40. Megginch Castle: *Rob Roy*; 41. Mugdock Country Park: *Shallow Grave*; 42.Newliston House: *The Little Vampire*; 43. Overtoun House, Milton: *Regeneration*; 44. Paisley: *Young Adam*; 45. Perth: *Young Adam*; 46. Pittenweem: *The Winter Guest*; 47. St Abbs Head: *Link*; 48. St Andrews: *Chariots of Fire*; 49. Saltcoats: *Late Night Shopping*; 50. Sheriffmuir: *Monty Python and the Holy Grail*; 51. Sma' Glen: *Chariots of Fire*; 52. Strathearn: *Country Dance*; 53. Stirling Castle: *Gregory's Two Girls*, *Kidnapped* (1971), *Tunes of Glory*; 54. Tantallon Castle: *Kuch Kuch Hota Hai*; 55. Traquair House: *Tam Lin*; 56. Trossachs: *Geordie*, *Rob Roy – The Highland Rogue*; 57. Union Canal: *Young Adam*

CHARIOTS OF FIRE (1981)

St Andrews is recognised throughout the world as the home of golf and its club was formally given the title 'Royal and Ancient' in the first half of the nineteenth century. It is one of cinema's great ironies that town and club should figure in an Oscar-winning film about athletics. It is, however, par for the course that St Andrews was simply playing a part, that of Broadstairs in Kent where the athletes trained for the 1924 Olympics. *Chariots of Fire* opens with barefoot athletes running across the West Sands to the triumphal music of Vangelis, a scene that sets the mood of the film, a true story that celebrates such traditional British virtues as amateur sportsmanship and Christian principle. The athletes actually run past the famous clubhouse when they leave the beach.

It is to the credit of actor Ian Charleson and the film-makers that they manage to present Eric Liddell, a Scot who refused to compromise his religious beliefs by running on Sunday, as a hero rather than an unbearable prig, building up the tension by contrasting his preparations with that of rival Harold Abrahams (Ben Cross), a Jew from Cambridge. Liddell is seen handing out prizes and running in the Sma' Glen, north of Crieff in Perthshire. Stewarts-Melville rugby ground at Inverleith in Edinburgh provided the location for the Scotland–Ireland athletics meeting where he preaches to the crowd in the rain, comparing faith to running a race, and Heriot's ground at nearby Goldenacre was the scene of the Scotland–France international, where Liddell is knocked over and still wins. Liddell is also seen running to a religious meeting in the Assembly Hall on the

Mound and he walks with his sister in Holyrood Park. Broughton McDonald Church in Broughton Place served as the Church of Scotland church in Paris, and the Café Royal at the east end of Princes Street was used as the London restaurant where Abrahams enjoys a romantic dinner.

The film took its title from a line in William Blake's 'Jerusalem': 'Bring me my chariot of fire!'. In the end Liddell and Abrahams both won gold. (So too did Douglas Lowe, but he did not really fit the storyline.) The film won gold at the Oscars as well, for best picture (in preference to *Raiders of the Lost Ark*), original screenplay, music and costumes. The triumphal tone continued when writer Colin Welland informed his largely American audience: 'The British are coming', a curious comment on the back of a film that already seemed an anachronism. The film undeniably contained some memorable moments, not least Charleson pushing his chin towards the finishing line, arms thrown back. *Chariots of Fire* gave the Edinburgh-born actor his one truly significant role. He died of AIDS in 1990.

ROBBIE COLTRANE

After years of patiently building a career on stage, in television and in British movies, the burly actor found a new worldwide audience through two huge movie franchises – *James Bond* and then, even more significantly, *Harry Potter*. Born Anthony McMillan in Rutherglen in 1950, the son of a doctor, he attended Glenalmond public school and studied at Glasgow School of Art before pursuing a career as a comic actor. He changed his name to Coltrane in homage to his sax-hero, developed a close association with writer and artist John Byrne, and was in

Robbie Coltrane in *Harry Potter* (Warner Bros)

the original production of his most celebrated play *The Slab Boys* in 1978. He was part of TV's seminal post-modernist Comic Strip troupe, along with Dawn French, Jennifer Saunders, Adrian Edmonson and Rik Mayall; and his fledgling big-screen career survived appearances in not one but two of the biggest British flops of the 1980s – *Revolution* and *Absolute Beginners*. Roles as Bob Hoskins's sidekick in the thriller *Mona Lisa*, and as Falstaff in Kenneth Branagh's *Henry V*, displayed his gentle charm to telling effect. He won the first of several Bafta awards for his performance as Glasgow rocker Danny McGlone, 'Big Jazza', in Byrne's TV mini-series *Tutti Frutti*; and a comedy double act with Eric Idle in ecclesiastical drag in *Nuns on the Run* cemented his reputation for comedy. However, it was the role of Fitz, the moody criminal psychologist in the television series *Cracker*, that really secured his status as a household name in Britain. 'A Dostoevskian central hero of Falstaffian attitudes,' said one critic. At over 6 ft and several hundred pounds in weight, Coltrane casts a giant shadow. He proved so popular as former KGB agent and likeable rogue Valentin Zukovsky in *GoldenEye* that he was recalled for a second outing with 007 in *The World is Not Enough*, and he was author J.K. Rowling's personal choice for Hagrid, the bearded giant who lives on the edge of the woods in *Harry Potter and the Philosopher's Stone*. Coltrane ensured Hagrid was one of the film's most fully realised creations, following Rowling's advice to imagine him as 'one of those really big Hell's Angels that gets off a motorbike and then starts talking about how his garden is coming along', which just about sums up Coltrane's appeal. His characters' bark, and certainly their appearances, have often been much worse than their bite.

SEAN CONNERY

As James Bond and latterly as an Oscar-winning actor and unofficial spokesman for his native land, Sean Connery became the most famous Scot in the world. He has been a controversial expatriate, an even more controversial advocate of Scottish independence and, despite rather than because of his services to Scottish politics, he finally became Sir Sean Connery. He has a personal fortune running into tens of millions and several luxury homes, but Thomas Connery was born in 1930 into a life of poverty. Working-class Irish stock, his father was a labourer, his mother a cleaner, and they lived in a two-room tenement flat at 176 Fountainbridge on the western fringe of Edinburgh city centre. The address long ago disappeared beneath the expanding Fountain Brewery, though a small section of old stone tenements survives on the corner of Fountainbridge and Grove Street. They look charming now, but Connery's home had no bath, a toilet was shared with other families, and his first bed was a drawer at the bottom of his parents' wardrobe.

Connery was never destined for further education: he left school at 14 and joined the navy, but was invalided out. A succession of jobs included life-guard, coffin-polisher and art school model, where students considered it beneath them to talk to him. Connery was in London to compete in the Mr Universe competition in 1953 when he learned a touring production of *South Pacific* was looking for muscular young men as sailors. Connery was muscular and had been a sailor, and so he found himself on the first rung of the ladder to fame and fortune.

Sean Connery in *Highlander* (20th Century Fox)

He appeared on stage, in television and in several films before getting the chance to play 'secret agent' James Bond in *Dr No*. If nothing else, it would provide him with a nice little jaunt to Jamaica, though Ian Fleming was horrified at the idea of this hairy, working-class Scot playing his gentleman spy. The author imagined Roger Moore or David Niven in the role, and they would in due course both play it, but Connery was right for the times. Fleming created Bond in the 1950s as a remnant of the Empire, but the films were a product of the 1960s when society was opening up for likely lads like Connery. His Bond was a new type of hero: vicious, but charming and witty with it, a character who enjoyed high society but seemingly came from outwith the crumbling English class system. By 1965 and the release of *Thunderball*, the fourth Bond film, Connery was the top box-office attraction on both sides of the Atlantic.

He alternated Bond with other films that would stretch him as an actor, including Hitchcock's *Marnie* in which he is a rich businessman who catches an employee robbing the safe and offers her the choice of jail or marriage. However, Connery found it increasingly difficult to dissociate himself from James Bond. He quit after *You Only Live Twice*, only to be lured back for *Diamonds are Forever* in 1970, for which he received a then astronomical $1 million which he used to set up the Scottish International Education Trust. Fine work in the mid-1970s included *The Offence*, in which he played a police officer with hidden demons, and *The Man Who Would be King*, an adaptation of a Rudyard Kipling ripping yarn with a wonderful double act of Connery and Michael Caine as two adventurers on the make on the Indian north-west frontier. However, even his best films were struggling to find an audience and *Cuba*, *Meteor*, *The Next Man* and *The Man with the Deadly Lens* suggested a career in terminal decline.

He returned to the role of Bond for the seventh and final time in *Never Say Never Again*, a 1983 remake of *Thunderball*, which signalled a revival in his fortunes. It was followed by *Highlander* (one of only four Connery features to shoot in Scotland – the others being *From Russia With Love*, *Five Days One Summer* and *Entrapment*). In *The Name of the Rose* he was a medieval Franciscan monk-cum-detective, investigating a series of murders with the inner strength of a man seeking greater truths in a relentlessly bleak world of dirt, disease and religious tyranny. He won an Oscar for best supporting actor for his performance as Jim Malone, an Irish-American cop with a Scottish accent in *The Untouchables*.

Many actors find it difficult to come to terms with the ageing process, but Connery seemed to relish it, playing father to Harrison Ford in *Indiana Jones and the Last Crusade*, though Ford is only 12 years younger. Connery had effectively become a major film star twice over, once in the 1960s as a dark and dashing leading man, and again in the 1980s when he redefined himself as a wise elder statesman of thrillers, dramas and action movies, a cross between his younger self and Yoda from *Star Wars*. He still figures in polls of the world's sexiest men at an age when other men are drawing their pensions and director Steven Spielberg famously said that he was one of only seven genuine film stars in the world.

BILLY CONNOLLY

Billy Connolly worked as a welder in the shipyards of his native Glasgow before becoming a folk singer, complete with banjo and beard. He played in the Humblebums with Gerry Rafferty (who later had a big solo hit with 'Baker Street'). Connolly became famous not so much for his music as for his caustic observations of life and scatological humour which filled the gaps between songs. Ultimately, the gaps were more popular than the songs and Connolly found fame as a stand-up comedian. Chat-show appearances gave him a UK-wide audience and viewers south of the border were knocked out by this hairy and uncouth, yet witty, Glaswegian. Celebrity status, a messy divorce and the media spotlight led to a difficult relationship with Scotland and the Scots, particularly in Glasgow,

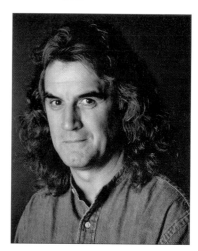

where many not only knew him but claimed to be funnier and resented his fame, fortune and marriage to Pamela Stephenson, former *Not the Nine O'Clock News* comedienne turned psychotherapist.

His story took an unexpected turn in the 1990s with a belated career as a film star in demand with British and Hollywood producers. Connolly had appeared in films and TV plays before, but often as variations on himself or in roles close to home. As early as 1975 he could be seen in *Just Another Saturday*, a play about sectarianism in Glasgow. Other roles followed in Anthony Shaffer's Gothic thriller *Absolution*, lightweight comedies *Water* and *Bullshot*, and the 1990 thriller *The Big Man*, in which Connolly was bare-

Billy Connolly, picture courtesy of Tickety-Boo Ltd

knuckle fighter Liam Neeson's sidekick. The film had a strong cast and the backing of Britain's Palace Productions and Miramax in the US but it flopped despite high expectations. *The Big Man* was an overwrought piece of hokum – had it worked, the Scottish film boom might have happened earlier.

Connolly played a Scottish teacher in the hit American sitcom *Head of the Class*, which led to the spin-off series *Billy*. He was Billy Bones opposite a bunch of puppets in *Muppet Treasure Island* and provided one of the voices in Disney's *Pocahontas*, but the turning point in his career was *Mrs Brown*, the 1997 film that started life as a BBC Scotland drama and went on to international acclaim and success on the big screen. There was no trace of the familiar insistent joker in his dignified and authoritative performance as a loyal retainer, providing support for a queen shattered by the death of her husband. There was even talk of an Oscar nomination and there was certainly more range in his work after that: he was a criminal who bore more than a passing resemblance to Glasgow gangster Jimmy Boyle in *The Debt Collector* and an angel in *Gabriel and Me*. Connolly, who had lived for years in Los Angeles, also seemed to make his peace with Scotland, buying Candacraig estate in Aberdeenshire, enjoying the role of laird and inviting Hollywood chums Steve Martin and Robin Williams to the local Highland Games.

JAMES COSMO

James Cosmo first appeared in movies in the late 1960s and early 1970s, in supporting parts in *Battle of Britain*, *The Virgin Soldiers* and *Young Winston*. A big,

James Cosmo in *Billy and Zorba*
(Ideal World)

burly individual, he seemed particularly suited to military roles and could play action man, gentle giant or straightforward heavy. Few films were shooting in Scotland at the time, but Cosmo, who was born in Dumbarton and has lived for much of his life in the Glasgow area, did get the chance to make his mark in 1986 in the fantasy adventure movie *Highlander*, as Angus MacLeod, kinsman to the immortal hero Connor MacLeod (Christopher Lambert). He also appeared in a wide range of Scottish television productions, including *Take the High Road*, *Brond*, *Rab C. Nesbitt* and *Roughnecks*. As a familiar Scottish face, he was well placed to win roles in the two most important films shot in Scotland in the 1990s, *Braveheart*, in which he was Mel Gibson's lieutenant Campbell, and *Trainspotting*, which provided him with an unusually subdued role as Ewan McGregor's dad. Subsequently, he was a key figure in the Inverness film studio initiative and attempts to bring Robert Burns to the big screen.

BRIAN COX

Although his greatest triumphs have been on the stage, Brian Cox has earned himself a distinguished entry in any book on modern film actors. Six years before Anthony Hopkins's Oscar, Cox won glowing reviews as the original Hannibal Lecter, or Lektor as it was then, in *Manhunter* (1986), which unfortunately suffered a botched release because of its producer's financial problems. He has been described as 'Scotland's answer to Marlon Brando', as much for his bulk and presence as for his acting style. He was the only actor to appear in both *Braveheart* and *Rob Roy*, and subsequently became a familiar face in Hollywood studio movies. Born in Dundee in 1946, the son of a weaver and a spinner, Cox left school at 15 and took a job sweeping the floor of Dundee Rep. He attended drama school in London and by his early 20s was appearing in leading roles in the West End. His most celebrated roles include Lear, and during the 1980s he won Olivier awards for *Rat in the Skull* and *Titus Andronicus*. Although he played Trotsky in *Nicholas and Alexandra* way back in 1971, his film career only really took off after *Rob Roy* and *Braveheart*. Well-paid supporting roles in *Chain Reaction*, *The Long Kiss Goodnight*, *For Love of the Game*, *Super Troopers* and *The Rookie* cross-subsidised parts in theatre and smaller independent films. He won several awards for his sensitive portrayal of a paedophile in *L.I.E.* and has been back to Scotland in recent years to film *Complicity*, *A Shot at Glory*

Brian Cox (Scottish Screen)

(as manager of Rangers Football Club), and *Strictly Sinatra*, though they failed to repeat the success of his two Scottish historical movies.

ALAN CUMMING

The Scot who makes Graham Norton seem like a shrinking violet has worked with some of the biggest names in showbiz, including the Spice Girls (playing documentary-maker Piers Cuthbertson-Smyth in *Spice World*), Stanley Kubrick (a brief but memorable appearance as a hotel desk clerk in Kubrick's swansong *Eyes Wide Shut*) and Britain's greatest film legend James Bond. In *GoldenEye* he was the obnoxious computer genius Boris Grishenko, the Russian agent who helps the Janus crime syndicate hijack the *GoldenEye* space weapons programme. 'I am in-vincible!' he proclaims triumphantly before an ocean of liquid nitrogen transforms him into a statue. Cumming left school in Carnoustie, near Dundee, at 16, and worked on a teen magazine before going to the Royal Scottish Academy of Music and Drama. He tasted early success with a role in the Scottish soap opera *Take the High Road* and as one half of the comedy double act Victor and Barry with Forbes Masson, later recycled in the sitcom *The High Life*. A camp variation on the boy

Alan Cumming, picture courtesy of ICM
(International Creative Management)

next door, he became a regular fixture on Scottish television and could easily have settled for the role of the new Rikki Fulton. Instead, he moved to London with then-wife Hilary Lyon, worked with the Royal Shakespeare Company, and won glowing reviews as Hamlet while rehearsing for the musical *Cabaret* during the day. He would go on to win a Tony award and a huge amount of press attention for *Cabaret* on Broadway. When Annette Bening presented him with the award, he handed her his bottle of water to hold while he made his speech. The film world opened up after his appearance in *Circle of Friends* with Chris O'Donnell, Minnie Driver and Saffron Burrows, with whom he was romantically involved for a while – he later announced he was bisexual. This was followed by *GoldenEye* and Jane Austen's *Emma*, in which he was the pompous and effete Reverend Elton. The screen lights up when his features appear, and he has proved incredibly versatile in terms of material, seeming equally at home with the Flintstones and Shakespeare. He brought all the relish and flamboyance of his *Cabaret* stage triumph to the decadent young emperor Saturninus in *Titus*, looking and acting like a cross between a New Romantic and a Nazi officer, a wonderfully camp, entertaining and yet entirely apt characterisation. His output has bordered on the workaholic – the live-action version of the cartoon *Josie and the Pussycats*, the ill-fated *Get Carter* remake, and *Spy Kids*, a surprise international hit in 2001. Hollywood studio movies enabled him to undertake more personal projects. *The Anniversary Party*, a collaboration with Jennifer Jason Leigh, gave him the chance to co-write, co-produce and co-direct, as well as star in an ensemble drama about a day in the life of a Hollywood couple. Cumming is never going to be a conventional romantic lead, nor will he ever be just another face in the crowd. He could play a Bond villain, but never Bond.

FINLAY CURRIE

Every fan of old movies will be familiar with the craggy features and white hair of Finlay Currie, the former Morningside choirmaster and organist who became one of the most sought-after character actors of the 1940s and 1950s. He was Biblical wise man Balthasar in the Oscar-winning epic *Ben-Hur*, St Paul in *Quo Vadis?*, pirate Billy Bones in *Treasure Island* and John Brown (the character later played by Billy Connolly) in *The Mudlark*. Born in Edinburgh in 1878, he was in his 60s before his film career took off. Playing organ for a production of *Henry IV* had led to a career in theatre, and he and his wife toured music halls as Currie and Courtney. He appeared in several Scottish films, including neglected minor masterpiece *The Brothers*. This period melodrama follows the arrival of a young Glasgow woman in a Skye community where transgressors are sent bobbing out to sea, tied up with floats and a fish on their head – the fish attracts a seabird that will dive down and pierce fish and skull together, an execution as ingenious as anything the modern horror films or ancient tyrants could devise. Currie could be saintly or sinister. His performance in David Lean's *Great Expectations* as the convict Magwitch, who surprises the young hero in a graveyard, remains the stuff of nightmares.

BETTE DAVIS

The legendary star of *Now, Voyager*, *All About Eve* and *What Ever Happened to Baby Jane?* visited Mull for location shooting on *Madame Sin*, a 1972 oddity that aimed to cash in on the craze for secret agent movies created by James Bond. Robert Wagner was agent Anthony Lawrence (and executive producer) and Davis, who was in her mid-60s by this time, was a variation on Dr No, an evil genius operating from a remote Scottish hideaway. Her scientists have been working on a machine that manipulates thoughts and memories, and she plans to steal a Polaris submarine which is undergoing tests nearby. Glengorm Castle served as her base and the film-makers also used Tobermory and other locations on Mull, and Crinan on the mainland. But while James Bond, Dr No et al. earned their chapter in movie history, Anthony Lawrence and Madame Sin remain nothing more than an obscure footnote.

DIRECTORS

While more and more Scottish stars have become household names, or at least familiar faces, comparatively little attention has been paid to those behind the cameras, particularly film directors, who supervise and often put their own personal imprint on the work that ends up on cinema screens. In the 1990s, Peter Mullan and Lynne Ramsay graduated from Scotland's short film schemes to write and direct features, but Bill Forsyth had to virtually create an industry when he started making comedies twenty years earlier, while Sandy Mackendrick was a staff writer at Ealing Studios in London before persuading his bosses to let him make *Whisky Galore!* on Barra in 1949. Directors often had to go to London or Hollywood to get started, and until relatively recently even keen film fans would struggle to name more than a handful of Scottish directors.

However, that does not mean there were no Scots directing films. The most celebrated Scottish director in Hollywood before the Second World War was Frank Lloyd. Not exactly a name that sparks instant recognition, but the Glaswegian directed the Clark Gable version of *Mutiny on the Bounty* (1935), and won two of the first six best director Oscars for *The Divine Lady* (1929) and *Cavalcade* (1933). On the second occasion, the host simply said: 'Come on up and get it, Frank,' and Capra bounded forward, only to see the triumphant Lloyd arriving from the other side.

Sandy Mackendrick was born in Boston, but his family were Scots and he grew up in Glasgow and attended Glasgow School of Art. *Whisky Galore!* (1949) and *The Maggie* (1954), which shot largely on Islay, were instrumental in developing cinema's image of canny Scots. Back in the US he made *Sweet Smell of Success* (1957), a film

Bill Forsyth (left) with David Puttman (Scottish Screen Archive)

whose reputation has grown considerably over the years. Lindsay Anderson was born in India, but considered himself Scottish, though *This Sporting Life* (1963) and *If . . .* (1968) were studies of two distinctly English institutions – rugby league and public school life. Donald Cammell, however, was born in the very heart of Edinburgh's historic Old Town, in the Outlook Tower beside Edinburgh Castle. He was an established painter and bohemian socialite when he wrote and co-directed *Performance* (1970). He subsequently went to Hollywood, though only a few of his scripts made it to the screen before he committed suicide in 1996.

John Mackenzie moved to London because of the lack of opportunities in film and television. He directed the archetypal London gangster movie *The Long Good Friday* (1980) and subsequently worked in Hollywood, though he returned to Scotland for several television dramas. Around the same time the two Bills, Forsyth and Douglas, determined they would make a stand on home turf. With the help of the British Film Institute, Bill Douglas wrote and directed the *My Childhood* trilogy (1972–8), an unsentimental portrait of a boy from a Scottish mining village. Bill Forsyth's movies were as whimsical and amusing as Douglas's were austere. He worked in information films before making *That Sinking Feeling* (1979) with £6,000, Glasgow Youth Theatre and lots of goodwill. His next film, *Gregory's Girl* (1981), sowed the seeds of a local industry, providing work for many individuals who went on to careers in films.

Mike Radford, another Indian-born Scot, taught at Edinburgh's Stevenson College before going to National Film School in England. He returned for *Another Time, Another Place* (1983), about Italian POWs on the Black Isle, and later worked in the US and Italy, where he directed *Il Postino* (1994). Gillies MacKinnon and Michael Caton-Jones also emerged from National Film School in the 1980s. Caton-Jones made an impact with *Scandal* (1989), and helped create the Scottish film boom with *Rob Roy* (1995). MacKinnon contributed *Small Faces* (1995), which drew on his adolescence in Glasgow in the 1960s, and *Regeneration* (1997), a portrait of shell-shocked war poets in Edinburgh. Peter Mullan took time off from acting to write and direct *Orphans* (1998), a comedy about bereavement with a distinctly black, Glaswegian sense of humour. David Hayman was another Glasgow actor who developed a parallel career as director. His films include *Silent Scream* (1989), and *The Near Room* (1995). Lynne Ramsay and Paul McGuigan both came to film via photography. Like MacKinnon, Ramsay drew on memories of growing up in Glasgow for her debut feature *Ratcatcher* (1999). Ironically, when Paul McGuigan directed the hard-hitting drama *Gangster No 1* (2000), he was hailed by its star Malcolm McDowell, as 'the English Scorsese'. The comment, intended as a compliment, neatly illustrates a problem of perception that Scots directors have sometimes faced when working outside Scotland.

DOCUMENTARIES

Scotland has a distinguished history in documentaries. Edinburgh International Film Festival was founded as a festival of documentary films and the very term 'documentary' was devised by a Scot, John Grierson. Born in Deanston, Perthshire, he wrote, produced, directed and edited *Drifters*, the 1929 film that helped define the concept, with its 'creative treatment' of Scottish fishermen. Grierson headed the Empire Film Board and GPO Film Unit, whose productions included the famous *Night Mail* (1936), a collaboration with composer Benjamin Britten and poet W.H. Auden, and he served on the Films of Scotland Committee which was responsible for most of Scotland's post-war cinema documentaries. Projects were financed by sponsorship and some were nothing more than glorified adverts, though *Seawards the Great Ships*, for which Grierson wrote the outline, won an Oscar

Seawards the Great Ships (Templar Films)

in 1962. The format virtually disappeared from cinemas in the 1980s to be reinvented on the small screen, though Kevin Macdonald, brother of *Trainspotting* producer Andrew Macdonald, was an Academy Award-winner in 2000 for *One Day in September*, a documentary feature about terrorist killings at the 1972 Olympics.

KIRK DOUGLAS

Few names sound more Scottish than Kirk Douglas, but it was all a sham. Born Issur Danielovitch to illiterate Russian immigrants in Amsterdam, New York, the young actor followed Hollywood practice and dumped his 'foreign-sounding' name in favour of something solidly Anglo-Saxon, or in his case Celtic. This cleft-chinned scion of the Douglas clan proved hugely adaptable, playing van Gogh in *Lust for Life*, Doc Holliday in *Gunfight at the OK Corral* and the title role in *Spartacus*. He came to Scotland for the secret agent movie *Catch Me a Spy* (1971), shooting on the Ballachulish ferry. It was written by Dick Clement and Ian La Frenais, who were better known for their sitcoms such as *The Likely Lads*. Sadly, this early attempt to move onto the big screen could not claim to be another *Spartacus*.

EDINBURGH LOCATIONS

1. Assembly Hall: *Chariots of Fire*; 2. Broughton McDonald Church: *Chariots of Fire*; 3. Café Royal: *Chariots of Fire*; 4. Calton Road: *Mary Reilly*, *Trainspotting*; 5. Edinburgh Academy: *The Prime of Miss Jean Brodie*; 6. Edinburgh Castle: *The Debt Collector*, *Main Solah Baras Ki* (*I Am Sweet Sixteen*); 7. Edinburgh University: *Journey to the Centre of the Earth*, *Jude* (as Christminster, Thomas Hardy's fictionalised version of Oxford); 8. Filmhouse: Edinburgh Film Festival HQ; 9. Fountainbridge: childhood home of Sean Connery; 10. Grassmarket: *Hold Back the Night*, *The Prime of Miss Jean Brodie*; 11. Greyfriars Churchyard: *Jude*, *The Prime of Miss Jean Brodie*; 12. Heriots' rugby ground: *Chariots of Fire*; 13. Holyrood Park: *The Battle of the Sexes* (as the Highlands), *Chariots of Fire*, *Restless Natives*; 14. The Mound: *The Battle of the Sexes*, *Restless Natives*, *Women Talking Dirty*; 15. New Town: *The Battle of the Sexes*, *Jude*, *Gregory's Two Girls*, *Shallow Grave*; 16. Newcraighall: *My Childhood*; 17. Newhaven: *Restless Natives*; 18. Niddrie: *The Acid House*; 19. Outlook Tower: birthplace of Donald Cammell, writer and co-director of *Performance*; 20. Princes Street: *Restless Natives*, *Trainspotting*; 21. Royal Mile: *Jude*, *Mary Reilly*, *Restless Natives*, *Women Talking Dirty*; 22. Scotland Street: *Shallow Grave*; 23. *The Scotsman* building, North Bridge: *Complicity*; 24. Stewarts-Melville rugby ground: *Chariots of Fire*; 25. Wester Hailes: *Restless Natives* (See page 30 for map)

EDINBURGH INTERNATIONAL FILM FESTIVAL

It has neither the glamour nor the weather to rival Cannes, but Edinburgh's comparatively modest film festival is recognised as one of the best in the world. The inaugural event took place in 1947, making Edinburgh the oldest continually running annual film festival in the world . . . technically. Cannes and Venice are older, but took a while to get going again after the Second World War. EIFF started as a documentary event, a sideshow to the new international arts festival, but soon expanded its remit. During the late 1960s and 1970s, it built an international reputation by leading the reassessment of genre film-makers, such as Sam Fuller and Roger Corman, and by championing the work of young directors like Scorsese and De Palma. John Huston called it 'the only festival worth a damn' and the organisers have been quoting him ever since. It can be haphazard, but it is also small, and that is one of its strengths. I had lunch with Clint Eastwood in the Caledonian Hotel when he came for *White Hunter, Black Heart* in 1990. He wanted to try a Scottish dish, not haggis, and I persuaded him to try cranachan, a mixture of cream, oatmeal and raspberries – he kept a press conference waiting while the chef prepared it and told me of his desire to make one final definitive western. It

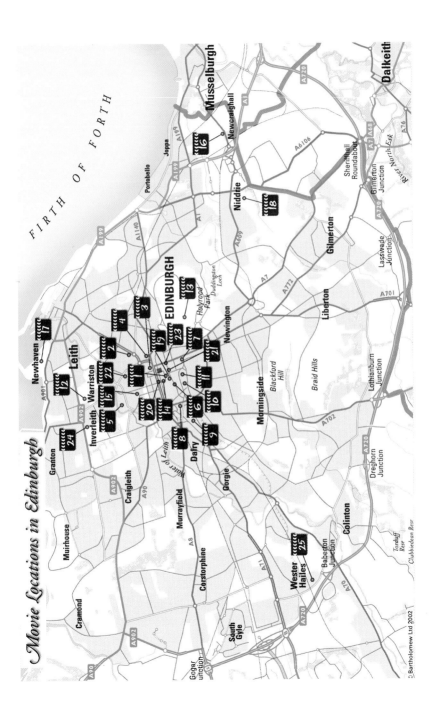

Movie Locations in Edinburgh

was called *Unforgiven*. The public can attend discussions with film-makers and the occasional A-list star at the Filmhouse, the former church in Lothian Road that is now the hub of the Festival. In the delegate centre or Cameo bar, would-be film-makers can rub shoulders with the real thing, pretend they are the real thing, and perhaps even become the real thing. The year after I had lunch with Eastwood, John Hodge, a junior hospital doctor from Glasgow, turned up at the festival with the outline for a blackly comic thriller he had scribbled on napkins, envelopes and other scraps of paper. Andrew Macdonald told Hodge he was a film producer – though general production assistant would have been a more accurate description – and that he could turn the script into a hit movie. Macdonald did get Hodge's script made and the film was called *Shallow Grave*.

ENIGMA (2001)

Robert Harris's novel about war-time spies and code-breakers was set largely around the top secret Bletchley Park base in Buckinghamshire and reached its climax with a shoot-out between hero and villain outside Northampton. The film, which starred Scotland's own Dougray Scott as the tormented code-breaker genius, along with Kate Winslet and Saffron Burrows, opted for a more dramatic backdrop, relocating the denouement to Loch Feochan on a rugged stretch of coastline south of Oban, and turning the shoot-out into a duel between a U-boat and the RAF. The cottage in those scenes also figured prominently in the much-loved otter movie *Ring of Bright Water* 30 years earlier.

ENTRAPMENT (1999)

Originally it was intended to shoot *Entrapment* mainly in the US, but Sean Connery was producer as well as star and he was able to direct his writers towards a Scottish setting for this thriller that bears more than a passing resemblance to *The Thomas Crown Affair*. Connery plays Robert MacDougal, 'Mac', a fabulously wealthy playboy suspected of a series of daring art thefts, pursued by insurance investigator Catherine Zeta-Jones. The big robbery sequences take place in New York, England and, on the stroke of the new millennium, Kuala Lumpur; but whenever Mac wants a little peace and quiet to recuperate or to plan his next adventure he retreats to Duart Castle, the ancient MacLean stronghold on Mull. It was a small indication of Connery's determination to be part of the Scottish film boom, and it was his first film in Scotland since *Highlander* in the 1980s. The castle also appears in *I Know Where I'm Going!* and *When Eight Bells Toll*.

CRAIG FERGUSON

When Craig Ferguson first appeared at the Edinburgh Festival he was so hard up he slept in the photo booth in Waverley Station. However, he found an appreciative audience for his stand-up routine in the nearby Café Royal and built an enthusiastic following with his bigoted character Bing Hitler. Before long he had his own television show and was up there with Billy Connolly at the top of the biz, before it all went horribly wrong with drink, drugs, divorce and the inevitable critical backlash. He headed for Los Angeles in 1995, starting over with ten-minute spots in clubs. His career took off again with a regular role, as a department-store boss, in the popular sitcom *The Drew Carey Show*. The script specified an 'a★★hole' – it was Ferguson's decision to make him English. That led to the film *The Big Tease*, in which he wrote, produced and starred. It's a wonderful comedy about a camp Glaswegian in a three-piece tartan suit who flies out to Los Angeles, with a documentary team in tow, thinking he has been invited to compete in the world hairdressing championship. The film draws on Ferguson's own experiences, turns the macho image of Scotsmen upside down, and remains one of the most underrated Scottish films ever. It shot in Glasgow and Los Angeles, and brought Ferguson back to the Edinburgh Festival in 1999 when he stayed in a VIP suite in the Balmoral Hotel, overlooking the station. Often journalists remember meeting stars, even if the star cannot quite place the journalist, but as far as I was concerned, I had never met Ferguson before yet he remembered me interviewing him for a paper in Cumbernauld, near Glasgow, where he grew up and played drums in a local band called Exposure. It was his first time, so apparently it was very special to him. His father was a postman, his mother a teacher, but despite fairly humble beginnings, his brother became Head of News at Scottish Television and one of his sisters, Lynn, became a leading comedienne. And here he was on his third career – rock star, stand-up comic and now Hollywood movie star. *The Big Tease* failed to fulfil predictions that it was the new *Full Monty*, but Ferguson bounced back the following year with *Saving Grace*, again taking on the triple role of writer, producer and star. It was a *Whisky Galore!* for the new century, with marijuana instead of whisky, and Cornwall instead of the Hebrides. He plays a gardener who encourages widow Brenda Blethyn to grow cannabis on an industrial scale to clear her debts and save her cottage. He also co-starred with Jane Horrocks and Catherine McCormack in the romantic comedy *Born Romantic*.

TOMMY FLANAGAN

A former painter and decorator and part-time disc jockey, Tommy Flanagan has become one of the most familiar Scottish supporting actors in cinema today. He has appeared in films as diverse as the Hollywood epic *Gladiator*, as Russell Crowe's servant Cicero, and Lynne Ramsay's Scottish arthouse hit *Ratcatcher*, in which he was the father who risks his life to save a drowning boy one minute and abuses his wife the next. Flanagan's own background is one of poverty, deprivation and violence, growing up in Easterhouse in Glasgow, and he started acting only after being attacked outside a pub and ending up scarred from ear to ear. Close friend Robert Carlyle encouraged him to take it up, and Flanagan spent three years with Carlyle's Raindog Theatre Company before Mel Gibson gave him his big film break in *Braveheart*. He played Morrison, the groom who revenges himself on the English lord who claimed feudal sexual rights from his bride. Flanagan's scar was to prove a selling point for hard-man roles in Hollywood, where actors usually pride themselves on perfect looks, and he appeared in *The Saint* as a character called Scarface, *Face/Off*, and *Plunkett and Macleane* with his old mate Carlyle.

LAURA FRASER

Laura Fraser was originally up for the role of the fair maid in the medieval romp *A Knight's Tale*. It might have seemed ideal casting for the wide-eyed Glaswegian billed in *The Man in the Iron Mask* simply as 'bedroom beauty' but it is typical that Fraser should end up not as Heath Ledger's lover, but as his blacksmith, for Fraser has long delighted in not doing the obvious. Born in 1975, she enjoyed a liberal middle-class upbringing. Her parents, a civil engineer and a lecturer, encouraged her artistic ambitions and indulged her during some wild teenage years. 'One night I came home with tyre marks on my legs,' she was once quoted as saying. 'I couldn't figure out what had happened.' She dropped out of the Royal Scottish Academy of Music and Drama after making her feature debut in *Small Faces*, Gillies MacKinnon's acclaimed drama about Glasgow gangs in the 1960s. No one could question her range of films, though the quality was decidedly uneven, ranging from the lame teen comedy *Virtual Sexuality*, in which she uses a computer to

Laura Fraser, picture courtesy of ICM (International Creative Management)

create a mate, to *Titus*, an adaptation of the Shakespeare play that makes *Reservoir Dogs* look like *Postman Pat*. Her character is raped, has her tongue cut out and hands chopped off. Fraser admits it was an enormous psychological strain, but she managed to hold her own in a cast that included Anthony Hopkins and Jessica Lange. A role as a spotty teen in Harry Enfield's *Kevin and Perry Go Large* represented another change of pace. Then, for *A Knight's Tale*, she learned to shoe a horse. Maybe horseshoes seemed preferable to tyres.

GLASGOW LOCATIONS

1. Anderston Cross bus station: *Restless Natives*; 2. Barras: *Restless Natives* (as New Mexico); 3. Britannia Theatre of Varieties and Panopticon (now closed), 117–19 Trongate: Stan Laurel's stage debut; 4. Buchanan Street bus station: *Trainspotting*; 5. Canniesburn Hospital: *Trainspotting*; 6. Clyde Tunnel: *Pyaar Ishq aur Mohabbat* (*Love, Love and Love*); 7. Crosslands Bar, Queen Margaret Drive: *Trainspotting*; 8. Finnieston: *Death Watch*; 9. Firhill basin, Forth and Clyde Canal: *Ratcatcher*; 10. Firhill complex, Hopehill Road: *Trainspotting*; 11. George Hotel (demolished), Buchanan Street: *Trainspotting*; 12. George Square: *Pyaar Ishq aur Mohabbat*; 13. Glasgow Central Station: *Late Night Shopping*; 14. Glasgow City Chambers: *Heavenly Pursuits* (as the Vatican), *The House of Mirth*; 15. Glasgow University: *Pyaar Ishq aur Mohabbat*, *You're Only Young Twice*; 16. Govan: *Ratcatcher*, *Trainspotting*; 17. Hampden Park: *A Shot at Glory*; 18. Jaconelli's café, Maryhill Road: *Trainspotting*; 19. Kelvingrove Art Gallery: *The House of Mirth*; 20. London Road Tavern: *Trainspotting*; 21. Necropolis: *Death Watch*; 22. Nitshill and Darnley: *Trainspotting*; 23. Partick: *My Name is Joe*; 24. Rouken Glen: *Shallow Grave*, *Trainspotting*; 25. Ruchill: *My Name is Joe*; 26. Springfield Quay: *Pyaar Ishq aur Mohabbat*; 27. Theatre Royal: *The House of Mirth*; 28. Townhouse Hotel (closed), West George Street: *Shallow Grave*; 29. Variety Bar, Sauchiehall Street: *Late Night Shopping*; 30. Volcano nightclub (demolished), Benalder Street: *Trainspotting*; 31. West George Street: *Pyaar Ishq aur Mohabbat*; 32. Whiteinch baths (closed): *Trainspotting*; 33. Wills' cigarette factory (now offices), Alexandra Parade: *Trainspotting* (See opposite page for map)

GREGORY'S GIRL (1981)

Rebel Without a Cause articulated the anger and frustrations of being a teenager in Los Angeles in the 1950s. A quarter of a century later another classic film captured the anxieties of Scottish youth. Leather jackets, switch-blade knives and suicidal car

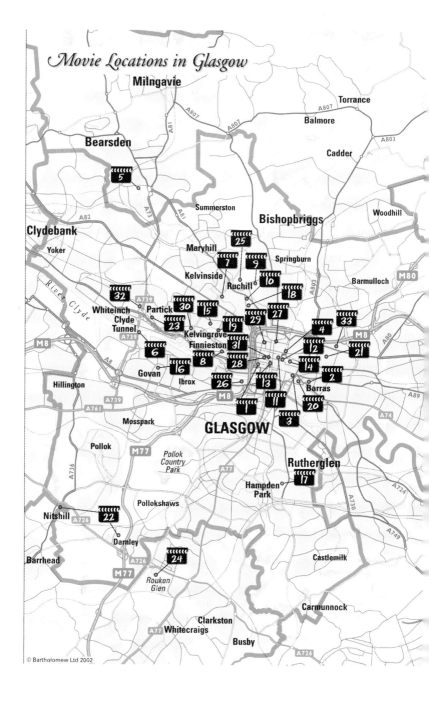

races were replaced by school blazers, cooking-class wooden spoons and suicidal football matches. *Rebel Without a Cause* had James Dean, *Gregory's Girl* had John Gordon Sinclair. Dean died young and became an icon, but Gregory was also an icon of sorts. This was Bill Forsyth's second feature, after *That Sinking Feeling*, and he used many of the same cast and crew. This time he had a low budget, instead of no budget; a memorably gawky lead in John Gordon Sinclair, in real life a holidaying electrician who could never quite decide in which order to put his names; and a beautifully measured script about Gregory's hopeless school football team, the girl who becomes its star and the romance that never quite develops between her and Gregory. The film is informed by a playful sense of humour, sometimes naturalistic and understated, sometimes totally surreal. What is that penguin doing wandering round the school? Many consider it to be Forsyth's best movie. It has often been praised for its innocence, yet it delivers voyeurism and nudity before the opening credits. The main location was Abronhill High School in Cumbernauld. The big old clock in the modern indoor town centre, where Gregory arranges to meet Dorothy (Dee Hepburn), came from St Enoch's Station in Glasgow.

Shortly after the film came out, Clare Grogan, who played Dorothy's friend Susan, became famous as the singer in the pop group Altered Images and her distinctive, screechy vocals figured prominently on the Top Ten hits 'Happy Birthday' and 'I Could be Happy'. But what is most remarkable about the *Gregory's Girl* alumni is the number who went on to make their mark in the movie business. Production supervisor Paddy Higson became a film and TV producer in her own right, and for a while had her own studio in Glasgow where she made the sub-Forsythian comedy *The Girl in the Picture*. Cinematographer Michael Coulter shot *Four Weddings and a Funeral* and was Oscar-nominated for *Sense and Sensibility*. David Brown, a 'runner' on *Gregory*, was production supervisor on *The Phantom Menace* and co-producer of *Enigma*. Pat Harkins, who played one of the schoolboys, was a propman on many films, including *Shallow Grave*, and went on to direct *The Final Curtain* with Peter O'Toole.

The belated sequel *Gregory's Two Girls* (1999) saw Gregory back at his old school as a teacher, not quite committing to a relationship with a colleague and lusting after a pupil. Gregory had gone precisely nowhere in two decades. It was a great and sometimes disturbing idea, but suffered from a feeble sub-plot involving ex-pupil Dougray Scott as a businessman exporting torture equipment. Cast and crew found Cumbernauld little changed. 'There was even a poster that was in the first film still in the classroom,' Sinclair told me. 'Then there was the chip shop that we used in the first film. It was the same lady who had owned it for 18 years. We said we wanted to go in and do some filming, and she said, "Oh, not again."'

GREYSTOKE – The Legend of Tarzan, Lord of the Apes (1984)

When Edgar Rice Burroughs created his classic story of an English orphan raised by apes in the African jungle, Lord Howard of Penrith offered to lend him the name Greystoke, so at least the boy would have some decent breeding behind him. The Howards own Greystoke Castle in the Lake District but the film-makers were unimpressed. So, for Tarzan's ancestral seat, they used Floors Castle, home of the Duke of Roxburghe, near Kelso. It is here Tarzan (Christopher Lambert) romances Jane Porter, though he resists the famous 'Me Tarzan, you Jane' chat-up line on this occasion. Floors is reputedly the largest occupied stately home in Britain, with 365 windows – one for every day of the year. The film shot largely on location in Cameroon and looks splendid, but it was an unhappy experience all round. Andie MacDowell played Jane, but was dubbed by Glenn Close. Robert Towne, the legendary screenwriter who won an Oscar for *Chinatown*, spent years on the script and wanted to direct it, but the job went to Hugh Hudson, fresh from the success of *Chariots of Fire*. Towne was so depressed with the end result he gave the writing credit to one P.H. Vazak, who happened to be his dog, so Vazak became the only canine Oscar nominee ever.

HAMISH MACBETH (1995–97)

Before *The Full Monty*, before even his wonderful turn as psycho Francis Begbie in *Trainspotting*, Robert Carlyle was already delighting a huge and faithful audience on BBC1 with his portrayal of the laid-back Highland policeman *Hamish Macbeth*. He stands for law and order in the village of Lochdubh (pronounced Loch-doo, meaning black loch), though he will happily partake of a joint and turn a blind eye to poaching, and is not above smashing a romantic rival's headlight and then booking him for the misdemeanour. Law and order, Hamish Macbeth-style, generally means protecting his little community against the evils of the outside world, and the ironic allusion to the classic westerns of Gary Cooper is made in the credits with the inclusion of a toy gun and sheriff's badge. Hamish is an able detective – when detective work is required, he takes a mature commonsense approach to policing – but he proves hopelessly incompetent when it comes to personal relationships and the rival claims of old flame Alex MacLaine (Valerie Grogan) and local reporter Isobel Sutherland (Shirley Henderson). If only they were as easy to please as his West Highland terrier Wee Jock, and subsequently Wee Jock Two, after the first Jock falls victim to a hit-and-run driver. There were three series which sold around the world, and they owed their success to Carlyle, to some imaginative plotting, a cast

Ralph Reiach and Robert Carlyle in *Hamish Macbeth* (photograph by Alan Wylie)

of weird and wonderful local characters and of course to the picturesque Highland locations. Plockton, at the mouth of Loch Carron in Wester Ross served as Lochdubh, and most of the filming was done in and around the village. It was built in the eighteenth century as a fishing village, though its neat, painted waterfront cottages are now used largely by holidaymakers and were easily accessible for the series. (It also featured in the film *The Wicker Man*.) Hamish's police house is the holiday cottage called Tullochard, so visitors can have the pleasure of living on location, while Rory Campbell's shop was Mackenzie's newsagent in the centre of Plockton. Interiors for the Lochdubh Hotel were shot at the Balmacara Hotel, the exterior was the private house at 43 Harbour Street, Plockton. Duncraig Castle was used as the production base; it provided various interiors and served as Zoot MacPherrin's mansion in the episode *West Coast Story*. Plockton Primary School and Plockton High both feature in the programmes, the former as the school, the latter as council offices and the like. Plockton is a small village and many locations are easily identifiable, and the locals will point visitors in the right direction. Shooting also took place at Kyle of Lochalsh, Duirinish, Drumbuie, Loch Achnahinich, Applecross and Skye. The major's house is Attadale House, Strathcarron. The beach in *No Man is an Island* is Camusdarrach in Morar, which also appears in *Local Hero*.

HAMLET (1990)

As a young man Franco Zeffirelli was fighting with partisans against the Germans in his native Italy when they ran straight into what he thought, or at least hoped, were Allied troops. Nervously, he asked if they were English. They indicated aggressively that they were not. Zeffirelli knew the fate that awaited captured partisans and thought he was about to die when one of the soldiers bellowed at him: 'We're no' f★★★in' English, Jimmy; we're f★★★in' Scottish!' Foreigners often think of the Scots as a regional variation on the English, but Zeffirelli would always remember the difference and Scotland and the Scots would always have a special place in his affections. He survived the war and became one of Europe's most distinguished film, stage and opera directors, taking Shakespeare to a new audience with his sexy young *Romeo and Juliet* in 1968. It was not until 1989, however, that he finally came to Scotland, searching for a castle for the film of *Hamlet* he planned to make with Hollywood superstar Mel Gibson. He had already considered the real Elsinore, Kronborg in Denmark, but felt it lacked the requisite menace. Dunnottar Castle, near Aberdeen had a long history of violence and bloodshed, and was now no more than extensive ruins on a clifftop, surrounded on three sides by the North Sea. Zeffirelli visited the site and announced that it was just what he wanted. He extended the ruins with an artificial facade and the castle appears as Elsinore in long shots and in the background behind Hamlet. Dover Castle was used for closer shots, and although most of the interiors were done at Shepperton Studios, Zeffirelli also filmed in the courtyard and in several rooms at Blackness Castle, a cold inhospitable establishment on a point on the Firth of Forth, west of Edinburgh.

JOHN HANNAH

John Hannah had been acting for more than ten years, in television, radio, commercials, and fringe and provincial theatre, when a supporting role in a modestly budgeted British comedy suddenly changed the course of his life. He was the quiet boyfriend to Simon Callow's flamboyant homosexual in *Four Weddings and a Funeral* in 1994. It became the most successful British film ever and gave Hannah one of the great scenes of British cinema, when he recites W.H. Auden's poem 'Stop All the Clocks' as a funeral oration. It was made all the more poignant by the way Hannah kept his emotions in check. 'Real people try to stop crying, whereas actors try to cry,' he said, tellingly, at the time. Suddenly Auden was back on the bestseller list and Hannah's career took off. Born in East Kilbride, near Glasgow, in 1962, the son of a toolmaker and cleaner, Hannah left school at 16 and worked as an electrician before going to the Royal Scottish Academy of Music and Drama. Despite his

John Hannah in *Rebus* (SMG)

working-class roots, *Four Weddings and a Funeral* helped define Hannah as a slightly dapper gentleman in the tradition of Cary Grant and David Niven, and there seemed little chance of him ever pipping Robert Carlyle, Peter Mullan or Brian Cox for a role as a Glasgow heavy. Hannah would have liked to have been in hard-hitting social dramas, but fate had pushed him in a different direction. With his bushy eyebrows and slightly lopsided face, he was hardly classic leading man material, yet he co-starred with Gwyneth Paltrow in the romantic comedy *Sliding Doors*. Changing pace again, he played the comic opportunist to Brendan Fraser's Indiana Jones type and Rachel Weisz's plucky Egyptologist in *The Mummy*, (and subsequently *The Mummy Returns*), which gave him a remarkable hat-trick of hits. He was one of the Canadians campaigning for Denzel Washington's release in *The Hurricane*, and he got the chance to play the English poet William Wordsworth in the fascinating British film *Pandaemonium*. He seemed now to have his pick of Hollywood and British films, but did not entirely turn his back on his native land. Through his own production company, Hannah developed several feature-length television dramas about Ian Rankin's detective *Rebus*, which shot in Scotland.

HARRY POTTER

Harry gets on a train at King's Cross Station in London and arrives hours later at a castle on top of a mountain. It does not take magical powers to work out where the schoolboy wizard might be. Although the setting is never made clear in the early books, geographical directions, landscape descriptions and author J.K. Rowling's own background all suggested Scotland. Rowling was born in Gloucestershire and lived in Portugal for a while, but settled in Edinburgh after the collapse of her marriage. A single mum on welfare, she famously wrote the first *Harry Potter* book in Nicolson's café in Nicolson Street because a cup of coffee was cheaper than heating her flat. *Harry Potter and the Philosopher's Stone* was filmed mainly on sets at Leavesden Studios in Hertfordshire, and at locations in the south of England, although Scotland provided background shots for several scenes. Harry and his friends get a fine view of the Glenfinnan area from the window of the Hogwarts express, and the climactic Quidditch match was superimposed by computer on a backdrop of Glen Nevis. The film-makers returned to Glenfinnan for *Harry Potter and the Chamber of Secrets*, and shot the Hogwarts express going over the famous viaduct.

DAVID HAYMAN

One of Scotland's most distinguished stage actors and directors, David Hayman has also become an increasingly familiar face in British films and Hollywood productions shooting on this side of the Atlantic, typically, but not always, as a close-cropped, mean-looking villain. His menace lies in his intensity, rather than physical bulk, and a sense that he might just be the genuine article. He was born in Glasgow in 1948 and worked in a steel works before going to the Royal Scottish Academy of Music and Drama. Celebrated roles during a long association with Glasgow's Citizens' Theatre included Hamlet and Lady Macbeth, and he gave a memorable performance as Glasgow gangster Jimmy Boyle in Scottish Television's *A Sense of Freedom* (1981). He was an obvious candidate for films shooting in Scotland throughout the 1980s and 1990s, and he duly turned up in *Eye of the Needle*, *Heavenly Pursuits*, *Venus Peter*, *Rob Roy*, *The Near Room* (which he directed), *Regeneration*, *My Name is Joe* and *The Match*. His most memorable roles include Sex Pistols manager Malcolm McLaren in *Sid and Nancy*, and he also appeared in *The Jackal*, *Vertical Limit* and *The Tailor of Panama*.

SHIRLEY HENDERSON

The diminutive, dark-haired Shirley Henderson had a small but memorable role in *Trainspotting* as Spud's girlfriend, a relationship that ends badly when he showers her family with the dubious contents of his bedsheets. When *Trainspotting* came out, Henderson was overshadowed by the younger, more glamorous Kelly Macdonald, but she has gradually established herself as one of Scotland's leading actresses on both the big and small screen. She was born in Forres in the north of Scotland in 1965, but moved to central Scotland as a toddler and was singing professionally in Fife working men's clubs while still at school. Like Ewan McGregor, she studied drama at Kirkcaldy College and Guildhall in London, and she appeared with Robert Carlyle in *Hamish Macbeth* before *Trainspotting*. Subsequently, she was a single mum in *Wonderland*, singer Leonara Braham in Mike Leigh's *Topsy-Turvy*, Bridget *Jones*'s friend Jude, David Suchet's daughter in the television adaptation of Trollope's *The Way We Live Now*, Steve Coogan's wife in *24 Hour Party People* and Moaning Myrtle, the ghost who haunts the girls' toilet in *Harry Potter and the Chamber of Secrets*. She was back in Scotland in 2002 for *Wilbur Wants to Kill Himself* and *16 Years of Alcohol*.

HIGHLANDER (1986)

Sean Connery has made few films in his native land and it is ironic that when he did get the chance to return to Scotland to make *Highlander* he should end up as an Egyptian-Spanish dandy, while the plum role went to Frenchman Christopher Lambert. *Highlander* began as a film-school writing assignment, after Greg Widen

visited Scotland on holiday. Connor MacLeod is one of a race of near-immortals, who can die only by chopping off each other's heads. He was born in the Highlands in the early sixteenth century, and driven out by suspicious clansmen when he recovered from what should have been fatal wounds. Connery's character Ramirez is another 'goodie' immortal who turns up as his mentor, but they are menaced by a 'baddie' immortal, the Kurgan. The film jumps back and forth in time and space, between ancient Scotland and modern New York. Audiences were confused by the structure, or maybe just the casting, but the film gained a new lease of life on video, and was followed by sequels and television spin-offs.

The original used numerous West

Highlander (20th Century Fox)

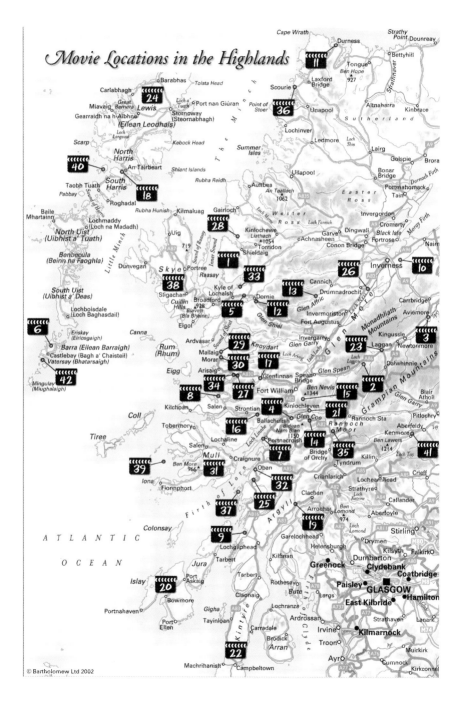

Movie Locations in the Highlands

© Bartholomew Ltd 2002

Highland locations and reinforced the image of Scotland as a wild mountainous country, populated by fierce warring tribes – a portrait that horrified cultural commentators. The sequels shot largely abroad, but Glenfinnan remains the Mecca of the *Highlander* cult, attracting devotees from all over the world. Bonnie Prince Charlie raised his standard there to start the 1745 Jacobite Rising, but for *Highlander* fans it is important as the birthplace of Connor MacLeod and his small-screen kinsman Duncan. *Highlander*'s Glenfinnan was constructed in the car park at Eilean Donan Castle, well to the north of the real Glenfinnan on Loch Shiel, although scenes of Lambert swimming and rowing were filmed at the real Glenfinnan, and the television series also shot there. It is from Eilean Donan in Wester Ross that the Clan MacLeod set out to battle at the beginning of the film, though Widen preferred the name Glamis, the name of the Queen Mother's ancestral home near Dundee and one of Macbeth's titles. Widen plundered Scottish history and geography for names, images and ideas he might hijack: his script says Connor and his wife 'leave Jedburgh and move east, settling on a farm outside Montrose', as if it were just down the road, rather than a fairly radical move from the Scottish Borders to a coastal town closer to Aberdeen than Dundee; the ancient equivalent of a move from Scotland to Australia.

Eilean Donan, with its causeway and loch, is one of Scotland's most picturesque locations, appearing in films as diverse as the James Bond film *The World is Not Enough* and the Bollywood spectacular *Kuch Kuch Hota Hai*, though its claims to authenticity are only slightly better than those of the film. A castle was built there in 1230, but was destroyed by the English in the eighteenth century and left in ruins for 200 years, at which point it was completely and expensively rebuilt. The film's big battle sequence was shot at Glen Coe, where the Campbells massacred the MacDonalds in 1692. MacLeod's keep was constructed at The Study, in Glen Coe; he is seen running on deserted sands at Refuge Bay in Morar; and he trains in swordsmanship at various locations from Mossy Wood at Arisaig to the Cioch pinnacle on Skye.

Of course, *Highlander* was complete fantasy, a mish-mash of history, mythology and science-fiction, but no one was pretending it was Shakespeare. It made Scotland look coolly dramatic and it attracted more visitors than many other Scottish films.

HIGHLANDS AND ISLANDS LOCATIONS

1. Applecross: *Laxdale Hall*, *Ill Fares the Land*; 2. Ardverikie: *Mrs Brown*, *Monarch of the Glen*; 3. Aviemore (as Russia): *The Duellists*; 4. Ballachulish: *Catch Me a Spy*, *Kidnapped* (1960); 5. Balmacara: *Hamish Macbeth*; 6. Barra: *Whisky Galore!*, *Rockets Galore!*; 7. Castle Stalker: *Monty Python and the Holy Grail*; 8. Castle Tioram: *Highlander III*, *Rob*

Roy; 9. Crinan: *From Russia with Love, Madame Sin, The Maggie*; 10. Culloden: *Culloden*; 11. Durness (as ancient Gaul): *Asterix and Obelix Take on Caesar*; 12. Eilean Donan Castle: *Bonnie Prince Charlie, Highlander, Kuch Kuch Hota Hai, Loch Ness, The Master of Ballantrae, The World is Not Enough, The Year of the Comet*; 13. Glen Affric: *Dog Soldiers, The Kidnappers*; 14. Glen Coe: *Bonnie Prince Charlie, Braveheart, Complicity, Highlander, Kuch Kuch Hota Hai, The Master of Ballantrae, Quest for Fire, Restless Natives, Rob Roy, The 39 Steps* (1935); 15. Glen Nevis: *Being Human, Braveheart, Harry Potter and the Philosopher's Stone, Highlander, Kidnapped* (1960), *Quest for Fire, Restless Natives, Rob Roy*; 16. Glen Tarbert: *Rob Roy*; 17. Glenfinnan: *Bonnie Prince Charlie, Charlotte Gray, Harry Potter and the Philosopher's Stone, Highlander, The Master of Ballantrae*; 18. Harris: *The Rocket Post, 2001: A Space Odyssey* (with Harris as Jupiter); 19. Inveraray: *Bullseye, The Three Lives of Thomasina*; 20. Islay: *The Maggie*; 21. Kinlochleven: *Braveheart, Rob Roy*; 22. Kintyre: *Death Watch, White Nights*; 23. Laggan: *Monarch of the Glen*; 24. Lewis: *Doctor Who, The Rocket Post*; 2 5. Loch Feochan: *Enigma, Ring of Bright Water*; 26. Loch Ness: *Loch Ness, The Private Life of Sherlock Holmes, Restless Natives*; 27. Lochailort: *Local Hero*; 28. Lower Diabaig: *Loch Ness*; 29. Mallaig: *Breaking the Waves*; 30. Morar: *Breaking the Waves, Hamish Macbeth, Highlander, Local Hero, Rob Roy*; 31. Mull: *Entrapment, Eye of the Needle, I Know Where I'm Going!, Madame Sin, When Eight Bells Toll, The Year of the Comet*; 32. Oban: *The Bridal Path, Morvern Callar, Ring of Bright Water*; 33. Plockton: *Hamish Macbeth, The Wicker Man*; 34. Polnish: *Breaking the Waves, Local Hero*; 35. Rannoch Moor: *Complicity, Quest for Fire, Rob Roy, Trainspotting*; 36. Scourie: *Being Human*; 37. Seil Island: *Ring of Bright Water*; 38. Skye: *Bonnie Prince Charlie, Breaking the Waves, The Brothers, Captain Jack, Dragonslayer, Flash Gordon* (at Breakish airfield), *Hamish Macbeth, Highlander, The Wicker Man, Monty Python and the Holy Grail*; 39. Staffa: *When Eight Bells Toll*; 40. Taransay: *Castaway 2000, The Rocket Post*; 41. Taymouth Castle: *Mrs Brown*; 42. Vatersay: *Whisky Galore!*

HONORARY SCOTS, DAVID NIVEN AND DONALD CRISP

David Niven always enjoyed a joke and it seemed wonderfully ironic that the archetypal Englishman was really a Scot, born in Kirriemuir, Angus – the same town as J.M. Barrie, creator of *Peter Pan*. As early as 1941, *The Scotsman* referred to him as a 'young Scots actor' and even his children believed he was born in Scotland. But the final punchline, revealed only after his death, was a birth certificate that showed he had been born at Belgrave Mansions, London. Niven was famous for embroidering stories, and studios were never slow to spice up their stars' biographies. Niven's father was Scottish, Niven served in the Highland Light Infantry and his biographer Sheridan Morley believed he simply considered

Scotland to be a more romantic birthplace than London. Niven's image was that of the English gent, *Bonnie Prince Charlie* aside, while Donald Crisp made a career out of Scottish character roles in Hollywood. If J.M. Barrie pioneered the sentimental 'kailyard' image of Scots and Scotland in literature, it was Crisp who promoted it on screen, in a series of films from *Beside the Bonnie Brier Bush*, in which he starred and directed in 1921, to *Greyfriars Bobby*, Disney's 'true' story of a dog that refuses to leave its master's grave, in 1961. Crisp maintained a lifelong pretence that he was from Aberfeldy in Perthshire, where a plaque was erected in his honour, and he kept his Scottish accent into old age. He was also supposedly a secret agent in Russia during the First World War – while making films in Hollywood at the same time! It was only long after his death that a Perth librarian proved that Crisp was a Cockney, born and bred.

THE HOUSE OF MIRTH (2000)

Edith Wharton's novel was set in suffocatingly polite New York society in the early twentieth century, but modern NYC was nothing like the city of a century ago. Director Terence Davies ruled it out as too busy and too expensive. He considered Philadelphia, Baltimore and Albany before making a quantum leap, right across the Atlantic, and settling on Glasgow. It was a little like the whole *Brigadoon* scenario in reverse, but Glasgow's grand Victorian buildings were thought to be closer to the

New York of the period than anything Davies could find, and afford, in America. It obviously helped that executive producer Bob Last was based in Scotland and had studied architecture at Edinburgh University. *The House of Mirth* shot at Glasgow City Chambers, Kelvingrove Art Gallery and Museum, and the Theatre Royal. Locations outside Glasgow included Gosford House near Edinburgh, and Manderston House in the Borders. It was a major change in direction for *X-Files*

Gillian Anderson in *The House of Mirth* (FilmFour)

star Gillian Anderson as Wharton's tragic heroine. She won glowing reviews and there was talk of an Oscar nomination.

I KNOW WHERE I'M GOING! (1945)

Michael Powell considered various islands off England and Wales before settling on Mull as the main location for his romantic drama. Joan Webster (Wendy Hiller) is on her way to marry an industrialist when she is halted by bad weather within sight of her intended destination. Forced to fill in time, she finds herself drawn to the local laird, Torquil MacNeil (Roger Livesey), but is determined not to let those feelings affect her plans. She finds shelter initially at Carsaig House (Erraig in the film), before moving to Torosay Castle (renamed Sorne by Powell), which is linked by a narrow-gauge railway to the ferry terminal at Craignure, a mile and a quarter away. Powell was determined to get his money's worth from his island location and Joan also visits Duart Castle and Moy Castle. Torquil was to have been played by James Mason but, according to Powell, he balked at the lack of first-class accommodation and was replaced by Livesey. In the end, Livesey was unable to go to Mull either, because of theatre commitments, and location shots of Torquil were done with a double and intercut with studio close-ups. Colonsay served as the island for which she was heading.

GORDON JACKSON

He was never exactly an A-list movie star, but Gordon Jackson was a familiar face in British films and television for half a century, achieving his greatest fame in middle age with two classic small-screen roles – as Hudson, the impeccable butler, in *Upstairs, Downstairs* (1970–75), and then as George Cowley, the gruff head of an anti-terrorist unit, in *The Professionals* (1977–83). Born in Glasgow in 1923, he performed in radio plays and trained as an engineering draughtsman. He was still in his teens, however, when he made his screen debut and developed his film career in parallel with a distinguished stage career that included work with Orson Welles and Alec Guinness. Often a rather meek character on the big screen, he was a hen-pecked son in *Whisky Galore!* and a patient suitor in *The Prime*

Gordon Jackson (SMG)

of Miss Jean Brodie. His most notable films include *Tunes of Glory* and *The Great Escape*. He appeared in several military roles, not as an action-hero, but invariably as someone's right-hand man or the voice of caution in the background.

JAMES BOND

James Bond was not only played by a Scot on screen, this lethal defender of the English Establishment was a Scot in Ian Fleming's original novels. His father was Andrew Bond of Glencoe, according to an obituary written by M and published in *The Times* when Bond is missing presumed dead in *You Only Live Twice*; his mother was Swiss. He apparently left Eton under a cloud after an incident with a maid, and enrolled at Fettes in Edinburgh, one of Scotland's most exclusive private schools. Ironically, the young Sean Connery delivered milk to the school, which counts Prime Minister Tony Blair among its old boys. Ian Fleming drew some of the details from his own background – he too attended Eton and there have been suggestions of an early departure because of an incident with a girl, and Fleming's grandfather was a wealthy Scottish banker. The second James Bond film, *From Russia With Love*, made an unexpected visit to Scotland after delays on location in the Balkans forced the postponement of the climactic motorboat chase. The budget was still very tight for the second film and it was decided it would be easier and cheaper to shoot it in Britain, so cast and crew relocated to Crinan in Argyllshire. The helicopter chase was shot in the hills above nearby Lochgilphead. Scotland appeared in its own right in *The World is Not Enough*, when the ever-popular Eilean Donan Castle in Wester Ross was decorated with masts and satellite dishes and figured as MI6's Scottish branch office. Among the gadgetry Q is developing there are bagpipes that also serve as a machine-gun and flame-thrower. Scotland also appeared in the 'unofficial' film of *Casino Royale* (1967), an overblown spoof that bore little resemblance to the other Bond films or the original novel. David Niven's Sir James Bond travels to Scotland, gets involved with the sinister Dr Noah (Woody Allen), and there is a grouse shoot with explosive robot birds. The film shot at the picturesque Perthshire village of Killin and elsewhere.

DEBORAH KERR

Deborah Kerr famously rolled in the surf with Burt Lancaster in *From Here to Eternity* and danced with Yul Brynner in *The King and I*. A Hollywood institution, she was nominated a record six times without a win for the best actress Oscar, before the Academy finally gave her an honorary statuette. She came from Helensburgh, which is usually cited as her birthplace, though she was actually born in a nursing home in nearby Glasgow. A genteel town on the north side of the Clyde, Helensburgh has probably contributed more to the screen industries than any other town of similar size in the world. John Logie Baird, the inventor of television, was born there and his boyhood neighbours included Jack Buchanan, who graduated from Broadway musicals to star in *The Band Wagon* with Fred Astaire. Andy Clyde, the grizzled sidekick in numerous westerns, grew up in Helensburgh, and director David MacDonald, whose films include *The Brothers*, was born there. Kerr trained as a dancer, initially at her aunt's school in Bristol, and made her debut in a Sadler's Wells production in her teens before turning to drama. Despite the beach antics with Burt Lancaster, she was more often to be found playing ladies, albeit sometimes troubled ladies, or religious paragons, beginning with a tour of duty in the Salvation Army in *Major Barbara* (1941). She worked for Powell and Pressburger on *The Life and Death of Colonel Blimp*, playing three different roles, and in *Black Narcissus*, as a nun, which led her to Hollywood and a starring role opposite Clark Gable in *The Hucksters*. Her record-breaking six unsuccessful Oscar nominations were for *Edward, my Son* (1949), *From Here to Eternity* (1953), *The King and I* (1956), *Heaven Knows Mr Allison* (1957), *Separate Tables* (1958) and *The Sundowners* (1960). Among her other films, *An Affair to Remember* is now regarded as a romantic classic, helped in no small measure by Meg Ryan's enthusiasm for it in *Sleepless in Seattle*.

KILT MOVIES, a brief history

Laurel and Hardy did it, the Australian actor George Lazenby did it in his single outing as James Bond, even ultra-cool Samuel L. Jackson did it – they have all worn the kilt in movies. Historians insist William Wallace would not have been seen dead in a kilt, but sales rocketed, particularly in the US, after Mel Gibson donned the kilt in *Braveheart*. Tartan and the kilt were a source of controversy long before *Braveheart*. They were banned after the 1745 Jacobite Rising, but the Lowlands went kilt-crazy early in the nineteenth century when Sir Walter Scott stage-managed the visit of a kilted King George IV to Edinburgh. Scott promoted the myth of the romantic Highlander in his fiction, including his novel *Rob Roy*. A century later, Harry Lauder played sell-out shows across America in a MacLeod tartan kilt, made several films, and surviving pictures show him arm-in-arm with Chaplin – Lauder in kilt and bonnet, Chaplin in bowler and baggy pants. Silent movies, including more than one take on *Rob Roy*, and early talkies gave the impression all Scots wore Highland dress. When John Ford took a break from Westerns to make *Mary of Scotland* he had Queen Katharine Hepburn greeted at Holyrood by a crowd in kilts singing 'Loch Lomond'. 'Straight off the shortbread tin,' was the considered verdict of George MacDonald

Fraser, historical novelist and author of *The Hollywood History of the World*. 'The film . . . may well be the worst historical picture I have ever seen.' At much the same time, Laurel and Hardy tapped into the kilt's comic potential when they joined the army in India in *Bonnie Scotland* and Hollywood's biggest star Shirley Temple succumbed to the charms of the tartan, playing a girl on another Indian military outpost in *Wee Willie Winkie*. One of cinema's greatest kilt moments occurs in yet another film set in India, when the Third Foot and Mouth Highlanders are ordered to 'up kilts', sending Afghan tribesmen fleeing in terror in *Carry on up the Khyber*. Mel Gibson more or less recreated the scene in *Braveheart* and got an Oscar for it. Lazenby's Bond wore a kilt in *On Her Majesty's Secret Service*. In the historical fantasy *Highlander*, Frenchman Christopher Lambert wore the kilt and Sean Connery had to make do with a fancy cap with a feather in it. Connery finally got the chance to wear both kilt and feathered cap in the ill-fated big-screen version of *The Avengers*, playing a mad villain who can control the weather. After *Braveheart*, it seemed everyone wanted to wear the kilt. Billy Connolly dressed up as Queen Victoria's Highland companion in *Mrs Brown*, Mike Myers got in on the act in *The Spy Who Shagged Me*, as Dr Evil's corpulent Scottish sidekick Fat Bastard, and Samuel L. Jackson wore a combination of kilt, knitted jersey, heavy boots and leather jacket when he played a drug dealer in *The 51st State*, sealing the kilt's rise from comic accessory to hip fashion statement.

LATE NIGHT SHOPPING (2001)

When Saul Metzstein and Jack Lothian decided to enter a competition to write a low-budget feature that could be shot in Glasgow, all they had was the title *Late Night Shopping*. They fleshed out a story about a group of young adults who hang out together in a late-night café. Ultimately, there was no place in the script for any shopping, but they stuck with the title anyway. Writer Jack Lothian drew from his own experience of life in a call centre and a supermarket, but the film is not the usual, down-beat, slice-of-life British drama. It relies heavily on the off-beat charms of its characters, including Sean (Luke de Woolfson), who hoped to become an astronaut but ended up a hospital porter, and Vincent (James Lance), a supermarket shelf-stacker who only ever dates women three times – 'three strikes and you're out'. It is like a Scottish *Friends*, with Glasgow instead of New York and, despite the disappointing box-office performance, rights were sold on to American television for a small-screen spin-off. None of the main characters in the film is played by a Scot, and the city is never named, reflecting director Metzstein's view that cities are losing their distinctive identities and allowing him to combine Glasgow locations with shots of the London skyline. The exterior of the cafe was the Variety bar in Sauchiehall Street, though the interior was a set. Metzstein also shot at Glasgow Central Station and at a Safeway supermarket in Bishopbriggs. When

James Lance, Heike Makatsch, Enzo Cilenti and Kate Ashfield
in *Late Night Shopping* (Ideal World / FilmFour)

the characters go to the seaside, it is to Saltcoats in Ayrshire, where Metzstein filmed at the crazy golf course and the Melbourne café.

STAN LAUREL

Stan Laurel was born Arthur Stanley Jefferson in Ulverston, Lancashire in 1890, but the family moved to Glasgow when he was a boy and he made his stage debut as a teenager in front of one of the city's notoriously difficult audiences, at the Britannia Theatre of Varieties and Panopticon in the Trongate. His father, A.J. Jefferson, was an actor, comic, director, producer, playwright and theatre manager. He took over the lease of the Metropole Theatre in Stockwell Street, Glasgow in 1901, though it seems it was a few years later before the family moved north. Post Office directories list the Jeffersons as living in Buchanan Drive, Rutherglen in 1905, while the address on Stan's mother's death certificate in 1908 is listed as 17 Craigmillar Road, and Stan is on record as saying he attended Rutherglen Academy, (which became Stonelaw High), and Queen's Park Senior Secondary. Jefferson later wrote an account of his son's stage debut: 'Without my knowledge, he had written himself a comedy music-hall monologue and, again without my knowledge, had prevailed upon a friend of mine

(A.E. Pickard), proprietor of a music hall in the city, to give him an opening date for a trial show.' By chance, Jefferson was passing the theatre, Pickard assumed he had come to see Stan and ushered him in. Stan was well received but his father was none too pleased that he had borrowed his topper, frock coat and trousers, and managed to ruin them in the course of his act. The premises were subsequently used as a shop, with the address 117–19 Trongate. Stan went to America with Chaplin and the famous Fred Karno company and joined the Hal Roach Studios, not as an actor, but as a director and deviser of gags. He directed Oliver Hardy in *Yes, Yes, Nannette!* (1925), which also starred pop-eyed Scot Jimmy Finlayson, who was to appear in about a third of Laurel and Hardy's 100 films, but *Putting Pants on Philip* (1927) is regarded as the first real Laurel and Hardy film. It was Stan who came up with the storyline of a kilted Scot (his character),who arrives to visit his American uncle (Hardy) and chases everything in a skirt. They were both in kilts in *Bonnie Scotland* (1935), when they go to Scotland to claim an inheritance and wind up in a Highland regiment in India.

JOHN LAURIE

John Laurie was almost 70 before he became a genuine screen star as the fatalistic undertaker and part-time soldier Private James Frazer, in the sitcom *Dad's Army*. But he made almost 100 films, had a distinguished stage career and served in both world wars. He was born in Dumfries in 1897, studied architecture, was wounded in the First World War and ended up guarding the Tower of London, in what sounds like a storyline straight out of *Dad's Army*. He actually served in the Home Guard in Paddington in the Second World War. He established himself as a leading stage actor in the 1920s, during which he played Hamlet and other major Shakespearean roles. He made his film debut in Hitchcock's *Juno and the Paycock* (1930), and had a small but memorable role as Peggy Ashcroft's mean-spirited crofter husband in *The 39 Steps*. A friend of Olivier, he appeared in his films of *Henry V*, *Hamlet* and *Richard III*. He often played Scots in English films, but was also a regular face in films set north of the border, turning up in *The Edge of the World*, *I Know Where I'm Going!* (on which he also served as ceilidh advisor), *The Brothers*, *Bonnie Prince Charlie*, *Floodtide*, *Treasure Island* (as Blind Pew), *Rockets Galore!* and *Kidnapped* (as Ebenezer Balfour). He appeared in the classic Korda adventure film *The Four Feathers*, and more or less reprised this role as a hostile tribesman in the *Dad's Army* episode *Two and a Half Feathers*. There were certainly some similarities between the actor and his most famous character. Laurie had supposedly dismissed *Dad's Army* as ridiculous nonsense, only to claim later that he always knew it would be a hit. The writers picked up on this trait and worked it into the character.

GARY LEWIS

Gary Lewis has one of the all-time great lines of Scottish cinema as the bereaved son in Peter Mullan's *Orphans*, hoisting the coffin on his back and proclaiming 'She ain't heavy, she's my mother' – a wonderfully surreal variation on the old Hollies hit. He grew up in Glasgow's tough Easterhouse scheme and worked as a street-sweeper when he left school. It was at a Young Socialists' meeting that he first met Mullan, who encouraged his interest in acting. Lewis was in his early 30s before turning professional. He worked with Robert Carlyle's Raindog Theatre Company, appeared in Mullan's shorts and made his feature debut as one of the prospective flatmates in *Shallow Grave*. He had no words, but was required to burst into tears when Ewan McGregor, Kerry Fox and Chris Eccleston interrogate him on his love life. Lewis built a reputation for his intensity and roles followed as Carlyle's mate in *Carla's Song*, Mullan's friend in *My Name is Joe* and a miner trying to do the best for his son in *Billy Elliot*, the hit film about a boy who wants to be a ballet dancer. Other films include *The Match*, *Gregory's Two Girls*, *Shiner* and Martin Scorsese's *Gangs of New York*.

THE LITTLE VAMPIRE (2000)

Carsten Lorenz could have been anyone when he turned up uninvited at a Scottish drinks reception at the American Film Market in 1999. He claimed to be a film producer looking for a country with great locations, a sense of antiquity and English as a first language. Lorenz and his partners had acquired the rights to *The Little Vampire* books, a series of bestsellers for children by German writer Angela Sommer-Bodenburg, with the reluctant vampires as the goodies. With an eye on the lucrative US market, they wanted an American boy at the centre of the story, but needed an Old World setting. Scotland proved ideal and the film used a combination of Scottish locations and German studio space. The title character was played by Rollo Weeks, with Richard E. Grant and Alice Krige hamming it up as his parents, and Jonathan Lipnicki as the American boy he befriends. Dunimarle Castle, by Culross in Fife, served as the exterior of Lipnicki's family's home – they were well-off – with interiors shot at Newliston House, just west of Edinburgh. Dalmeny House, on the Firth of Forth, provided exteriors for Lord McAshton's house, with Gosford House in East Lothian, and Dundas Castle at South Queensferry, providing interiors. The market scenes were shot at Culross and the countryside scenes were shot on the east coast, around Coldingham and Cockburnspath.

KEN LOACH and friends

Ken Loach was born in Nuneaton and *Poor Cow* and *Kes* made him a key figure in

Ken Loach (Scottish Screen)

English social-realist cinema in the 1960s, but *Riff-Raff* marked the beginning of a long association with Scotland in 1990. Although set largely on a London building site, it focused on a Scot, played by Robert Carlyle, and was written by Glaswegian Bill Jesse, who had worked on building sites but sadly died before the film was completed. There was some location shooting in Glasgow, and Loach returned to the city a few years later for *Carla's Song* (1996), in which Carlyle plays a bus driver who becomes involved with a Nicaraguan refugee and ends up in Central America. Paul Laverty, a former civil rights lawyer, sent the script outline to Loach on spec. He subsequently collaborated with Loach again on *My Name is Joe* and *Sweet Sixteen*, two festival hits that shot in Glasgow and the Greenock area respectively. Loach's regular

Martin Compston in *Sweet Sixteen* (Sixteen Films)

producer Rebecca O'Brien is also Scottish, and their experience encouraged their then-colleagues at Parallax Pictures co-operative to come to Scotland to make *The Governess* and *Hold Back the Night*. 'Everybody hates Tony Blair in Scotland, so this cheers us up enormously,' joked old-style socialist Loach. 'I find the people and their outlook very sympathetic, very congenial and, by and large, they still treat each other like human beings.' At the time of going to press Loach, Laverty and O'Brien are developing another Scottish film.

LOCAL HERO (1983)

Bill Forsyth made *That Sinking Feeling* and *Gregory's Girl* with tiny budgets and local teenagers as stars. But, for his third feature, he had the financial clout of David Puttnam and Goldcrest behind him and was able to recruit Hollywood legend Burt Lancaster to play the head of an American oil company that wants to build a refinery at Ferness Bay in the Highlands. Lancaster's character Happer sends one of his executives to Scotland to do the ground work, choosing MacIntyre (Peter Riegert) on the strength of his name. For the fictitious setting of Ferness, Forsyth wanted a location that would combine a picturesque village with an expanse of golden sands and he considered shooting on Lewis, in the Outer Hebrides, before logistic considerations finally forced him to settle for a combination of the tiny Aberdeenshire village of Pennan, a few dozen whitewashed houses on a narrow strip of land between cliffs and sea, and Camusdarrach Beach on the other side of the country at Morar. Even Denis Lawson's hotel was a combination of locations from east and west: a couple of houses in Pennan, with the addition of a suitable sign, were used for exterior shots, while interiors were shot at the Lochailort Inn, near Morar. Forsyth had been inspired by *Whisky Galore!*, and *Local Hero* attracted similar criticism from Scottish social commentators and critics, with accusations that Forsyth had abandoned sparky contemporary comedy in favour of couthy stereotypes, sentiment, nice scenery and a big-name Hollywood star. But the detractors completely missed the point: Forsyth builds stereotypes only to undermine them – the Highland idyll shattered by a low-flying jet, the remote wee village whose minister is black, the Scottish-American MacIntyre who turns out to have no Scottish connections, and most memorable of all, the bunny rabbit which Peter Capaldi rescues from the roadside, only for it to be served up to him at dinner. The film was a major commercial hit and fans from all over the world visited the locations, with many heading straight for Pennan's famous red telephone kiosk which MacIntyre uses to keep in touch with his boss, though the phone box in the film was a fake because the film-makers wanted it in a more exposed position. Ben Knox (Fulton Mackay) is the one man who refuses to sell out to the oil company. His tumble-down beach-house was at Camusdarrach. The cottage at the end of the beach was used as the church in the film, though interiors were shot at Our Lady of the Braes Roman Catholic church at Polnish, which was in use at the time but subsequently closed. (It also appears in *Breaking the Waves*.) The village shop was the shop at Pole of Itlaw, Banffshire, and the village hall, where the ceilidh takes place, was at nearby Hilton. Forsyth and his team encountered problems getting permission to use locations at both Morar and particularly at Pennan. 'There were days when I would get down on my knees and beg for the keys to a location which we'd already paid a lot of money for,' said

Peter Riegert and Christopher Rozycki in *Local Hero* (Enigma / Goldcrest)

location manager David Brown. The film's success brought hordes of tourists to Pennan and was a big money-spinner for the local Pennan Inn, but there were mixed feelings about the village's new fame. The producers of the TV drama series *2000 Acres of Sky* intended to use it as their main location, but difficulties in securing official permission forced them to go instead to Port Logan in Wigtownshire.

LOCH NESS (1995)

Nowhere in Scotland looked quite Scottish enough for Arthur Freed when he made *Brigadoon*, but Loch Ness was considered sufficiently vast and mysterious for the makers of this gentle family film exploring the myth of the loch's celebrated monster. Well, it was almost right. Ted Danson and Joely Richardson shot on location on Loch Ness, but the film-makers threw in a few extra shots from elsewhere to make it just a little more atmospheric. They wanted a picturesque lochside village with a pier, so they intercut Loch Ness with footage from the little village of Lower Diabaig on Loch Torridon, about 50 miles north-west along a precipitous single-track road. It is in one of the most spectacular parts of Scotland, with wild mountains towering over deep sea lochs. They also wanted a lochside castle. Loch Ness has a splendid sixteenth-century ruin, Urquhart Castle, which Billy Wilder used in *The Private Life of Sherlock Holmes* (1970). But the makers of *Loch Ness* decided it was not quite dramatic enough and, like many others, headed for Eilean Donan in Wester Ross. They also shot in Dores, Foyers and Fort Augustus, as well as in England and the US. Danson plays an American zoologist who comes to disprove the existence of the legendary beast, falls for hotelier Richardson, and also gets a few other surprises . . . Come on, they were never really going to make a family fantasy film in which the sceptical zoologist proves Nessie doesn't exist, were they? Or were they?

DAVID McCALLUM

One of Scotland's few genuine screen heart-throbs, David McCallum received more than 30,000 fan letters a month at the height of his fame. Although it was on TV that he achieved superstardom, he appeared in several dozen films. He was born in 1933 in Glasgow, where his father was leader of the Scottish Orchestra and his mother a cellist. He was only 13 when he began appearing in juvenile roles in radio drama. Early films include *A Night to Remember* and *The Great Escape*, after which he headed for Hollywood where his first role was as Judas Iscariot in *The Greatest Story Ever Told*. But other film roles proved elusive and he was reduced to appearing in the pilot episode of a James Bond imitation for television, playing a supporting role of a rather sullen Russian to Robert Vaughn's hero. However, McCallum's character Ilya Kuryakin proved so popular that the producers reconceived the series, with Kuryakin and Vaughn's Napoleon Solo as equal partners. *The Man from UNCLE* ran for 100 episodes between

David McCallum in *The Man from UNCLE* (Arena / MGM)

1964 and 1967 and the taciturn, blond-haired, polo-necked Kuryakin became the epitome of cool. The series was so popular that episodes were re-edited and released as feature films. McCallum never made the breakthrough as a Hollywood film star, but starred in a number of television series including *Colditz* and *Sapphire and Steel*. His youthful looks eventually faded and he turned up as a sleazy dentist in Michael Winner's *Dirty Weekend* (1993).

KELLY MACDONALD

Kelly Macdonald had been working as a barmaid in Glasgow when a friend gave her a leaflet inviting would-be actresses to open auditions for the female lead in *Trainspotting*. She had been thinking about drama school and reckoned an audition would be good experience, never entertaining the idea that she might actually get

Kelly Macdonald in *Gosford Park*
(Capitol)

the part. She had her photos taken in a booth on the way and almost turned back when she saw the other glamorous candidates, but she had exactly the raw talent and vitality, teenage sexuality and sense of mischief that director Danny Boyle wanted for the role of Ewan McGregor's schoolgirl seductress. With a sparkly little dress and a neat line in put-downs, Macdonald commands the screen from the moment the camera alights on her at the bar. Born in 1976, Macdonald grew up in the Glasgow area, except for a brief period living in a caravan near the picturesque town of Aberfoyle after her mother and father split up. After *Trainspotting* she went on to appear with Jessica Lange in an adaptation of Honoré de Balzac's *Cousin Bette*. She was still wading through the book during filming, but director Des McAnuff maintained she brought something to the part no one else could. 'Underneath her charm, beauty and sophistication, she exposes the demon in this girl,' he said. She found a ready supply of films on both sides of the Atlantic, even if some of these films had more difficulty in finding audiences. Some roles were strange – she worked in a Welsh bingo hall in *House!* – others were just disappointing. She sold cigarettes in a Glasgow casino in *Strictly Sinatra* and was little more than a face in the crowd in the Scottish country-house melodrama *My Life So Far*. Yet, she held her own alongside some of Britain's finest actors, with a nicely under-played performance as Maggie Smith's maid in Robert Altman's classy murder mystery *Gosford Park*. 'The still centre around which a glittering cast orbits,' cooed *Premiere* film magazine. The *Trainspotting* star was back on track.

ANGUS MACFADYEN

Angus Macfadyen may have been short of film experience when invited to audition as Prince Edward in *Braveheart*, but he was not short of self-belief, telling producer/director/star Mel Gibson that he should cast him not as the effeminate English prince, but as William Wallace's rival and eventual successor Robert the Bruce. He harangued Gibson for an hour and a half, forcing an unconditional surrender and getting the chance to deliver that wonderful address to the troops before the Battle of Bannockburn at the end of the film: 'You have bled with Wallace . . . now bleed with me.' Macfadyen's mannered performance as a man wrestling with inner demons contrasted well with Gibson's instinctive Wallace. Macfadyen was a man apart on set and off, finding little in common with his fellow actors: they came from Ireland and the west of Scotland, he came from Edinburgh; they came from working-class backgrounds whereas Macfadyen's father was a doctor for the World Health Organisation. He had gone to school in France and Denmark, and learned his craft in the bohemian atmosphere of the Edinburgh University Theatre Company, deciding on a play the evening before and staying up all night to rehearse. He saw *Braveheart* as his passport to Hollywood, but soon discovered not every film is an Oscar-winner, and not every role matched Robert the Bruce. He played a killer who thinks he is Hitler in *Snide and Prejudice* – tag-line 'He couldn't tell Reich from wrong', and he was warlord to kung-fu fighting kangaroos in *Warriors of Virtue*. Just when it looked like he might disappear without trace, his fortunes suddenly improved with the roles of Lucius in *Titus* and the young Orson Welles in Tim Robbins' star-studded *Cradle Will Rock*, a role his agent told him he had no chance of getting. Playing the boy genius as theatre director, Macfadyen drew on his experiences at Edinburgh University's Bedlam Theatre.

EWAN McGREGOR

Two kids go off on a family outing to the local cinema: *Star Wars*, the biggest hit of all time, has finally arrived at the Odeon in Perth. They are intrigued by the

Ewan McGregor, picture courtesy of Peters, Fraser and Dunlop

strange space creatures, fascinated by a story of heroes and villains and a space princess, excited by the lightsaber duel between the wise old knight Obi-Wan Kenobi and the wheezing black-clad Darth Vader, and totally blown away by the climax when the X-wing fighters attack the Death Star. Back home in Crieff, a quiet little town in the foothills of the Scottish Highlands, the youngsters re-enact the film with their lightsabers – two little boys with two little toys. The years pass and the boys grow up. Elder brother Colin fulfils his dream and becomes a fighter pilot, while George Lucas decides it is time for a new *Star Wars* movie and the younger brother, Ewan, gets the chance to become Obi-Wan Kenobi. It is the sort of plotting that might turn up in a novel and be dismissed as far-fetched. *Star Wars* played a major role in Ewan McGregor's decision to become an actor. It was not simply that it was the most exciting film he had ever seen, it was also because his uncle, Denis Lawson, was up there on the screen playing one of the X-wing fighter pilots. Denis saves Luke Skywalker's life and, subsequently Luke, guided by the voice of Obi-Wan Kenobi, destroys the Death Star. Denis was an occasional and exotic visitor to Crieff – he was an *actor* – and Ewan decided that that was what he wanted to be as well. 'I decided to become an actor, even though I had no idea what that meant,' he said later.

His parents were both teachers, and Colin was head boy at Morrison's Academy, the town's historic fee-paying school. It was little short of a local scandal when Ewan dropped out at 16 and took a job lugging sets around at Perth Theatre, making his professional acting debut as a turbanned extra in a stage production of *A Passage to India*. He did a foundation course in theatre arts at Fife College of Technology in Kirkcaldy, went to the Guildhall School of Music and Drama in London, and left early for a showy starring role in the Dennis Potter mini-series *Lipstick on Your Collar*, playing a War Office clerk who staves off boredom by staging musicals in his head. When Robert Carlyle passed on *Shallow Grave*, McGregor got the chance to play one of the greedy trio who hang onto their dead flatmate's money. The darkly humorous thriller possessed an energy, style and flair rare in British cinema. It marked the arrival not only of McGregor as a film actor (discounting a fleeting appearance in *Being Human*), but also of the exciting new film-making team of director Danny Boyle, writer John Hodge and producer Andrew Macdonald. But it was their next film that turned McGregor from a promising newcomer into an icon. Mark Renton had been one of an array of colourful young Edinburgh deadbeats in Irvine Welsh's novel *Trainspotting*, but he became the focus of the film, a nihilistic anti-hero for the times, outspoken and refreshingly honest. While Renton acknowledges that heroin brings 'misery and desperation and death', he complains that many ignore the pleasure it also gives. 'Otherwise we wouldn't do it. After all, we're not f★★★ing stupid.' McGregor brought just the right intelligence and arrogance to the role.

Although Renton might seem a galaxy away from the dignified Obi-Wan Kenobi, it was McGregor's performance in *Trainspotting* that was to lead to the meetings that landed him the role in *Star Wars Episode I: The Phantom Menace*, with the promise of starring roles in two more guaranteed blockbusters to maintain his international profile. There were times when it seemed as well that he had that guarantee to fall back on, as so many of his other films flopped. He had looked uncomfortable in the period drama *Emma*. *Brassed Off* bore some similarity to *The Full Monty*, but the idea of redundant workers getting their self-respect back by stripping for a paying audience was altogether sexier than redeeming themselves in a brass band. *The Pillow Book* was an arty indulgence, *The Serpent's Kiss* and *Nightwatch* disappeared without trace and *A Life Less Ordinary*, *Velvet Goldmine*, *Rogue Trader* and *Nora*, with McGregor as James Joyce, all failed to fulfil expectations. *Moulin Rouge*, Baz Luhrmann's audacious and strangely poignant reinvention of the musical, finally provided him with that increasingly elusive hit, playing the impoverished writer wooing the doomed Nicole Kidman with his reinterpretation of 'Your Song' and other anachronistic pop standards in the Paris of 100 years ago. He made an unlikely action hero in Ridley Scott's *Black Hawk Down*. *Star Wars Episode II: Attack of the Clones* made it three hits in a row. Sporting a fulsome beard, he was an older, wiser Obi Wan than he had been in *Episode I*. He also seemed constrained perhaps by the legacy left behind by Alec Guinness's performance in the earlier films. *Young Adam* brought him back to Scotland in 2002 and it was his first feature on home soil since *Trainspotting*.

MacGUFFIN

MacGuffin was the name Alfred Hitchcock gave to the secret plan or similar plot device that motivated his characters. The exact nature of it was of more interest to the characters than the audience. Everyone remembers Cary Grant being chased by a plane and hanging from Mount Rushmore in *North by Northwest*, for instance, but few remember the government secrets James Mason is trying to smuggle out of the country. Hitchcock once explained that the term came from a story about two men on a train going to Scotland: 'One man says, "What's that package up there in the baggage rack?" And the other answers, "Oh, that's a MacGuffin." The first one asks, "What's a MacGuffin?" "Well," the other man says, "It's an apparatus for trapping lions in the Scottish Highlands." The first man says, "But there are no lions in the Scottish Highlands," and the other one answers, "Well, then that's no MacGuffin."' In other words the ultimate nature of the MacGuffin is unimportant. Hitchcock attributed the story and the term to Angus MacPhail, co-writer of *Whisky Galore!* and *The Man Who Knew Too Much*.

KEVIN McKIDD

Trainspotting was not only the best British film of the 1990s, it was also the best poster, with Diane snarling, Sick Boy using his fingers as a gun, Spud looking daft in oversized glasses, Begbie giving a V-sign and Renton dripping wet, presumably back from his dip in the worst toilet in Scotland. You could argue that Tommy's absence was similarly symbolic as he dies from AIDS, an unlucky victim who tries drugs only after his girlfriend dumps him. The truth is more prosaic – Kevin McKidd had booked a holiday to North Africa which clashed with the photo shoot.

While others got the high-profile roles, the Elgin-born actor beavered away in modest British films, on television and stage, building his reputation gradually with a succession of impressive performances – a light-opera singer in *Topsy-Turvy*, Count Vronsky in Channel 4's adaptation of *Anna Karenina*, and the leader of a troop of soldiers menaced by werewolves in the Highlands in *Dog Soldiers*, (filmed mainly in Luxembourg, with establishing shots from Glen Affric). He seemed the most ordinary of the *Trainspotting* characters, but he made those qualities work for him and he was to emerge as one of the most versatile.

Kevin McKidd (photograph by Jeremy Hirsch)

MISSION: IMPOSSIBLE (1996)

The blockbuster cinema version of the television series from the '60s and '70s shot on location in the Czech Republic, Virginia and England, but the railway in the final scenes was in Nithsdale in the south-west of Scotland. The film-makers wanted open countryside with an absence of overhead power lines, so a second unit shot extensive footage on stretches of line between Dumfries and Annan, and Dumfries and New Cumnock, shooting from train and helicopter. A complicated plot, dubbed 'Mission Impenetrable' by some, reaches its climax on a train supposedly speeding towards the Channel Tunnel, when agent Ethan Hawke (Tom Cruise) catches up with traitor Jim Phelps (Jon Voight), fights him on the roof of the train, and ends up hooking Phelps's helicopter to the train, forcing it to follow the train into the tunnel. Cruise, however, never came to Scotland – he and Voight were acting against a 'blue screen'. George Lucas's visual effects specialists took the Scottish footage, added the train, helicopter and tunnel entrance, which were computer-generated, and then finally added the figures of Cruise and Voight to complete the stunning climax.

MRS BROWN (1997)

The close relationship between the recently widowed Queen Victoria and her Highland ghillie John Brown scandalised nineteenth-century society, and producer

Douglas Rae discovered it was still a highly sensitive subject when he made *Mrs Brown*. The queen had gone into a deep depression after the death of her husband Albert. She disappeared from public life and the future of the monarchy became the subject of national debate, even before her Scottish companion came on the scene. Before long there was even deeper concern about her relationship with Brown. He rode roughshod over courtiers and protocol, and some believed he had the sort of power over Victoria that Rasputin would later have over Tsar Nicholas and his wife Alexandra. The British monarchy, unlike their Russian cousins, did at least survive, but more than a century later there remained serious concerns about the subject and its possible offence to the Royal Family. Sean Connery had been mooted to play John Brown many years earlier, but the project was apparently scrapped because of royal disapproval. Neither the title *Mrs Brown*, nor the involvement of former shipyard welder and X-rated comedian Billy Connolly, would have done anything to allay fears. Moreover, those of a nervous disposition were unlikely to have been reassured by Connolly's original suggestion for the role of Queen Victoria – Bob Hoskins. The diminutive Cockney star of *The Long Good Friday* and *Who Framed Roger Rabbit* had impressed Connolly with a turn as Victoria at the Edinburgh Festival. Rae came up with the counter-proposal of Judi Dench. He was refused permission to film at many

Dame Judi Dench and Billy Connolly in *Mrs Brown* (Ecosse / BBC Films)

63

THE POCKET SCOTTISH MOVIE BOOK

of the genuine settings, though he did get to shoot ballroom scenes at Taymouth Castle near Aberfeldy, where Victoria had danced on her honeymoon. He used Duns Castle in Berwickshire, to represent Victoria's Highland castle at Balmoral in Aberdeenshire. The stables are those at nearby Manderston and the harbour is at Cockburnspath, also in Berwickshire. Rae did not shoot entirely in the Borders, however. The private Ardverikie estate, near Dalwhinnie in Inverness-shire, was used for the grounds of Balmoral. It was the beginning of a long association between Ardverikie and Rae's Ecosse Films, who returned there for the hit television series *Monarch of the Glen*. *Mrs Brown* also shot at the nearby River Pattack. Locations south of the border included Osborne House, Queen Victoria's real home on the Isle of Wight, and Wilton House in Wiltshire which doubled for Windsor. The film was conceived by Connolly and Rae while working together on a television series about Scottish art. They were discussing great Scottish characters Connolly might play in the wake of Mel Gibson's outing as William Wallace and Liam Neeson's Rob Roy. *Mrs Brown* started life as a modest BBC Scotland television drama, and shot in just 30 days on a budget of £1.5 million. The film proved respectful and entirely chaste. It was about a friendship rather than a scandal, with Judi Dench's sombre queen and Connolly's heavily bearded, straight-talking Highlander making a memorable and touching odd couple. With the financial muscle and showbiz nous of Miramax behind it, *Mrs Brown* became an international hit and Dench was nominated for an Oscar.

MONARCH OF THE GLEN (2000–)

Following the international big-screen success of *Mrs Brown*, Ecosse Films took on the daunting task of filling BBC1's prestigious Sunday night light-drama slot, previously occupied by *Hamish Macbeth*, and they came up with another winner in *Monarch of the Glen*. It was inspired by stories written 60 years earlier by Compton Mackenzie, author of *Whisky Galore!*. Like *Hamish Macbeth*, *Monarch of the Glen* revolved around the fortunes of a personable young Scot, who seemed more able at his job than his personal life and it was played out against similarly picturesque Highland locations. Alastair Mackenzie played Archie MacDonald, a young London restaurateur, recalled to the ancestral family home of Glenbogle believing his father is at death's door. It is Glenbogle that seems to be in terminal decline and Archie is persuaded to stay and use his business acumen to stall the banks and turn its finances around. For Glenbogle House, Ecosse used Ardverikie (1), a private house on Loch Laggan. They had used its estate for *Mrs Brown*. For Glenbogle itself, they used the nearby village of Laggan (2) on the River Spey, ten miles south-west of Kingussie, with the village school and store featuring pretty much as themselves though the names were changed. If visiting, make sure you

64

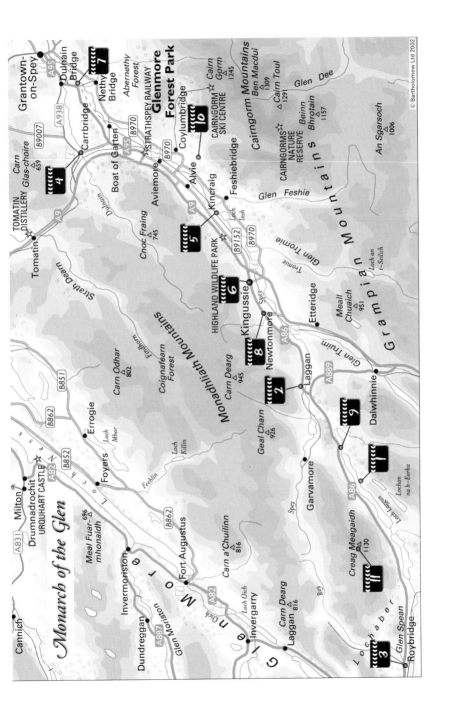

get the right Laggan – there are numerous places called Laggan scattered across Scotland and there is even another one on the Spey, further north in Morayshire. Cille Choirille Church, near Roy Bridge (3), served as the parish church, while public meetings were held in the village hall at Carrbridge (4), voting took place in Kincraig (5), the local council was based in Kingussie (6) and the station was Broomhill (7) on the Strathspey Steam Railway. Newtonmore (8) provided several locations, with the Clan Macpherson Museum serving as Glenbogle Tea Rooms. At one point or other, Archie seems to be romantically involved with just about every woman in the cast, except his mum. There is Justine, his original partner from London, the local schoolteacher Katrina with whom Archie has romantic moments at Pattack Falls (9) and Loch an Eilein at Rothiemurchus (10), the visiting banker Stella, and the housekeeper Lexie. Creag Meagaidh (11) was the mountain location for the dramatic hill race in the first series, when Archie blows his chance of victory by helping the injured Katrina. Archie's efforts to set affairs straight are continually thwarted by his eccentric, jovial father Hector (Richard Briers) and Hector's friend Kilwillie (Julian Fellowes, who wrote the period murder mystery *Gosford Park* while shooting *Monarch* and won an Oscar for best original screenplay). Over the course of several series, the programme-makers shot throughout Badenoch and Strathspey, which was 'rebranded' for marketing and tourism purposes as 'Monarch Country'. Foreign sales of the television series meant an international audience of 50 million, with many fans coming to visit locations. Occasionally the programme-makers ventured farther afield and in the episode in which grouse is flown to London, the helicopter flies over the monument, viaduct and loch at Glenfinnan, whose other screen visitors include *Highlander*'s Connor MacLeod and *Harry Potter*.

MONTY PYTHON AND THE HOLY GRAIL (1975)

So, there is nowhere in England that is quite English enough for those weird Monty Python people. Instead, they make a film all about King Arthur and his Knights of the Round Table in Scotland. And then they are praised not only for their surreal humour, but also for their realistic recreation of medieval England. Typical. And surreal. It is Doune Castle, near Stirling, at which King Arthur (Graham Chapman) presents himself at the beginning of the film. You remember the scene – he does not have a horse, but he does have a servant who simulates the sound of horses' hooves by banging two half coconut shells together. Arthur suggests the coconuts were brought to Mercia by migrant swallows and we are off on one of the silliest, wackiest adventures ever. It should have been called *Monty Python and the Attempt to Get Away from Doune Castle*, because Doune crops up throughout the film in various guises, including Camelot itself. The Pythons also filmed at nearby Sheriffmuir, scene of a Jacobite battle in 1715; at Arnhall Castle, Killin and Bracklinn Falls in Perthshire; and on Skye. The Bridge of Death, where the knights must answer three questions before crossing, was shot at the Meeting of the Three Waters in Glen Coe. Eventually, the knights believe they have reached the castle that holds the grail, for which the film-makers used Castle Stalker, a bleak fortress on a small island about 25 miles north of Oban. Just then the police turn up, arrest them and force the curtailment of filming. *Monty Python and the Holy Grail* has acquired a huge cult following over the years, with many fans visiting the original locations. Doune Castle has even lent visitors a set of coconut shells to provide sound effects during their tour.

MORVERN CALLAR (2002)

Lynne Ramsay drew heavily on her own experience of growing up in Glasgow for her short films and for debut feature *Ratcatcher*, but she tapped in to the Scottish

Samantha Morton in *Morvern Callar* (BBC/ Company Pictures)

literary renaissance for her second full-length film, an adaptation of Alan Warner's *Morvern Callar*. It follows the fortunes of two shop assistants who turn their backs on a grey existence in Scotland and go off clubbing in Spain. Samantha Morton, an Oscar nominee for Woody Allen's *Sweet and Lowdown*, was desperate to play the title character whose boyfriend slashes his throat on page one, leaving her a healthy bank balance and an unpublished novel, which she passes off as her own. The role of her best friend went to Kathleen McDermott, a trainee hairdresser from Glasgow, who was approached by the casting director while shopping in Glasgow's Argyle Street. Warner never names the town, but it is readily identifiable to anyone who knows it as Oban, and Ramsay shot on location there and in Almeria in Spain, as well as at Twickenham Studios.

PETER MULLAN

In the days before computer-generated imagery, Woody Allen made a very clever and amusing film called *Zelig*, in which the title character turns up at a succession of historic events in the first half of the twentieth century, ranging from a Nazi rally to a Scott Fitzgerald garden party. Peter Mullan is very much the Zelig of the Scottish film scene. When the flatmates fell heir to a case full of cash in *Shallow Grave*, it was Mullan who came looking for it. When Ewan McGregor wanted to score in *Trainspotting*, it was Mullan who sold him the drugs. When

Peter Mullan in *My Name is Joe* (Channel Four Films)

The Magdalene Sisters (Antonine PFP Ltd)

Mel Gibson took command of the Scottish army in *Braveheart*, there was Mullan poking fun at him because he was so short. Mullan used his acting fees to live on while writing and directing short films, before shorts became an established route into features. He made *Close* on his own doorstep for £500 in 1993 in which he played the over-protective father who takes extreme measures to get rid of the undesirable element in his stair. In 1998 he went to the Cannes Film Festival both as writer-director of *Orphans*, his debut feature, a deliciously black comedy-drama about bereavement, and as star of Ken Loach's *My Name is Joe*. Both were set in Glasgow, Mullan's home town since infancy, though he was born in Peterhead. His performance as a recovering alcoholic in *My Name is Joe* won him the best actor award, and prestigious film roles followed in *Miss Julie*, *The Claim* and *Young Adam*. His second feature as writer-director was *The Magdalene Sisters*, a drama focusing on the plight of 'immoral' young women, who were virtually imprisoned and used as slave labour by brutal nuns in Ireland's Magdalene asylums, as recently as the 1960s. Although set in Dublin, it shot in the Dumfries area, with the Old Convent in Maxwell Street as the principal location.

MUSIC

Scotland's contribution to film music has not been restricted to the bagpipes, though that contribution should not be underestimated – while researching this

Craig Armstrong (photograph by Peter Ross)

book, I came across an Internet site called 'The Bagpipes go to the Movies' and the Bs alone include *Backdraft*, *Battle of Britain*, *Bedknobs and Broomsticks*, *Bhowani Junction*, *Billy Liar*, *Blink*, *Bonnie Prince Charlie*, *Bonnie Scotland*, *Braveheart*, *Breaker Morant*, *Breaking the Waves*, *A Bridge Too Far*, *Brigadoon*, *The Buccaneer* and a Burger King commercial. *Moulin Rouge* owed a debt not just to the singing voice of Ewan McGregor, but also to Scots composer and arranger Craig Armstrong. He played with Glasgow band Texas and provided music for theatre before moving into films, working on Peter Mullan's early shorts and winning a BAFTA for *Romeo and Juliet*. As well as composing original music, Armstrong established a reputation for

69

orchestral and string arrangements, and he orchestrated the *Mission: Impossible* theme. *Moulin Rouge* presented him with one of his biggest challenges – rearranging pop standards for a film set a century ago, including 'Your Song' and 'Roxanne'. He won a Golden Globe for the film and was voted Bowmore Scottish Screen Film-maker of the Year. Other scores include *Plunkett and Macleane*, *The Bone Collector* and *Kiss of the Dragon*. On the other hand, Patrick Doyle began as an actor, appearing in *Chariots of Fire*, before developing his talents as a composer. He worked closely with Kenneth Branagh, acting in and composing the music for *Henry V*, *Dead Again*, (a particularly evocative score), and *Much Ado About Nothing*. Latterly, however, Doyle has concentrated on music and his scores include *Carlito's Way*, *Sense and Sensibility* (for which he received an Oscar nomination), *Bridget Jones's Diary* and *Gosford Park*.

MY CHILDHOOD: The Bill Douglas Trilogy (1972–78)

Bill Douglas's trilogy of autobiographical films hardly compares with *Braveheart* and *Trainspotting* in terms of box-office grosses, but many cineastes regard them as the best films ever to come out of Scotland. *My Childhood*, a mere 48 minutes long, presents a sparse portrait of a boy, Jamie, living in poverty in a Scottish mining village in the 1940s, with his half-brother Tommy and an elderly granny. A man, who may be Tommy's father, gives them a canary, but the cat eats it and Tommy beats the cat to death. Douglas was born in 1934 in the mining village of Newcraighall, on the eastern outskirts of Edinburgh, and it was to Newcraighall that he returned for filming. He depicts his world without sentimentality and with little dialogue, leaving the audience, like his protagonist, to work out what it means. Critics noted enthusiastically that *My Childhood* was a virtual return to silent cinema. *My Ain Folk* and *My Way Home* continue Jamie's story through to adolesence, national service in Egypt and some hope of a better future. Douglas died in 1991.

RAY PARK

Ray Park was plucked from the obscurity of stunt work to play one of the most recognisable characters in the movies when he was given the role of the villainous Darth Maul, with his red and black face complete with bald head and horns, in *Star Wars Episode I: The Phantom Menace*. Park was born in Glasgow in 1974 and lived near the Rangers' ground where he got into mischief as a wee boy climbing local buildings – a sign of things to come. His father was an electrician who had trouble finding work, so the family moved to London while Park was still a young child. Soon after the move, he took up martial arts and gymnastics, and by his mid-teens he was competing internationally. He taught martial arts before getting his film break as a stuntman on *Mortal Kombat 2: Annihilation*. Word spread quickly about his athletic fight moves and led to meetings with George Lucas and his stunt co-ordinator, and ultimately to the role of Darth Maul, though his voice was dubbed. He proved *Star Wars* was no one-off when he appeared as the evil mutant Toad in *X-Men*, another huge hit.

PETER PAN

It all began in Kirriemuir, Angus, where J.M. Barrie was born in 1860, the son of a weaver and the ninth of ten children. He found fame and fortune as a writer in London, and film producers beat a path to his door. There have been twice as many films of his stories as those of Sir Walter Scott, but many are marred by sentimentality and only *Peter Pan* retains its original popularity. The original play was staged in 1904, Disney released its classic cartoon version in 1953, and a belated sequel, *Return to Never Land*, was a hit in 2002. Steven Spielberg's *Hook* had Dustin Hoffman as Captain Hook, Julia Roberts as Tinkerbell and Robin Williams as an ostensibly grown-up Peter who has lost touch with his inner child. Barrie's story of a boy who never (usually) grows up and his orphan gang even spawned *The Lost Boys*, the cult 1987 film in which Kiefer Sutherland led a gang of young Californian vampires.

THE PRIME OF MISS JEAN BRODIE (1969)

Along with the romantic Highlands and proletarian Glasgow, this portrait of Edinburgh, in all its unashamed middle-class glory, deserves a place in any list of the crème de la crème of Scottish films. Miss Brodie sees herself as a beacon of culture in the stuffy traditional school where she teaches, but she is, in her own way, as narrow-minded and snobbish as anyone at the Marcia Blaine School for Girls, and much more dangerous, promoting not just the virtues of Italian Renaissance artists, but also of Italian fascism. Maggie Smith won an Oscar as the misguided Miss Brodie, and Rod McKuen's theme tune remains a dry-throated classic, but the film owes much to its Edinburgh locations, the spirit of which it captures perfectly even though many of the interiors were shot at Pinewood Studios. Novelist Muriel Spark lived in Bruntsfield Place and was educated at

Maggie Smith in *The Prime of Miss Jean Brodie*
(20th Century Fox)

nearby James Gillespie's School for Girls. One of the teachers, Miss Christina Kay, provided the model for Spark's Miss Brodie and the film's Jean Brodie lives just down the road at Admiral Terrace. Most of the drama, however, takes place at the school, with Donaldson's School for the Deaf in Henderson Row serving as Marcia Blaine's. The building was subsequently taken over by the adjoining Edinburgh Academy, a private fee-paying school, as exclusive as Marcia Blaine's. Miss Brodie takes her 'special girls' to Greyfriars churchyard, probably best known for Greyfriars Bobby, the dog who reputedly kept watch at his master's grave and was the subject of a popular Disney film. Miss Brodie and the girls also visit the Vennel, off the Grassmarket, which affords a fine view of Edinburgh Castle. Mr Lloyd (Robert Stephens), the art master, had his studio just across the street from Greyfriars, on the corner of Candlemaker Row and Merchant Street. His rival Mr Lowther (Gordon Jackson) invites Miss Brodie to his home in Cramond, a picturesque suburb on the Firth of Forth, though in the film his home turns out to be Barnbougle Castle, just along the coast on the Dalmeny estate – not bad on a teacher's salary. Curiously, St Trinian's, the antithesis of Marcia Blaine's and the setting for a series of comedies in the 1950s and 1960s, also has its roots in Edinburgh. The school, in which it seemed every junior was a violent hellcat and every senior a sex-mad strumpet, was inspired by St Trinnean's, an establishment famous for its radical ideas located at St Leonard's Hall, now part of Edinburgh

University's halls of residence beside the Royal Commonwealth Pool. Ronald Searle, who drew the cartoons that inspired the films, heard about it when stationed in Scotland during the Second World War. The real school, which had relocated to Galashiels, closed in 1946. Alastair Sim, who cross-dressed to great effect as the genteel headmistress in *The Belles of St Trinian's* and *Blue Murder at St Trinian's*, was born in Lothian Road, a short walk from the homes of Ms Spark and Miss Brodie and just across the road from where Miss Kay lived.

ROB ROY (1995)

Although the money came from Hollywood, *Rob Roy* was conceived, written and directed by Scots. It was the brainchild of Peter Broughan, a former BBC producer, inspired by a local legend that the famous outlaw had hidden in a tree in the old Stirlingshire village of Balfron where Broughan lived. While he found the initial story idea on his doorstep, Broughan had to go to New Zealand to track down the man he wanted to turn it into a script. Alan Sharp, a Scot, had made a big impact in Hollywood in the early 1970s before concentrating on lucrative and relatively undemanding work for American TV. Sharp made his name with westerns, including the classic *Ulzana's Raid*, and Broughan believed Rob Roy's story had many classic western elements such as big empty landscapes, landowners, cowboys, rustlers and long-haired cattle. Michael Caton-Jones, who directed *Scandal* and *Memphis Belle*, completed the Scottish triumvirate, with Irishman Liam Neeson in the title role. The Balquhidder area, where Rob Roy lived in the early eighteenth century, was ruled out as a location because of modern development and the spread of anachronistic pine plantings. The film-makers opted instead for the West Highlands, with their Rob Roy emerging as something of a multiple home owner – a stone cottage was built at Bracorina on the north side of Loch Morar, a plaster-house constructed on Rannoch Moor and a prefabricated dwelling airlifted to a remote location at Inversanda in Glen Tarbert. The film also shot at Glen Coe, in the hills above Kinlochleven, which provided the dramatic opening panorama, and in Glen Nevis, where the MacGregor village was built. However, filming of the ceilidh (party) scene, with 200 extras and 36 dancers, was washed out by heavy and sustained rain and it had to be re-done inside at the Perth Equestrian Centre. Nearby Drummond Castle served as the seat of the Marquis of Montrose (John Hurt), and was chosen for its ornamental terraced gardens though other unrelated scenes were also shot in the grounds. The cobbled courtyard of Megginch Castle, near Perth, was used as a village square and Crichton Castle, south of Edinburgh, was the exterior of the gambling den where Rob Roy and Archibald Cunningham (Tim Roth) have their duel. Roth was a wonderful villain – dandified and powdered, yet deadly and ultimately tragic. He won an Oscar nomination for the performance, and he and Neeson produce possibly the best sword fight ever seen on film; not mere acrobatics, but a true reflection of the nature of the two characters. Rob overdoes the lectures on honour, but Caton-Jones made excellent use of the Highland locations. Rob Roy, who was immortalised by Sir Walter Scott, had already been the subject of several previous films. *Rob Roy* was the first known 'story' film shot in Scotland in 1911, in a primitive studio at Rouken Glen on the outskirts of Glasgow, and on location in Rob Roy country around Aberfoyle. There was an American *Rob Roy* a couple of years later and an epic British version in 1922, shot in the Loch Lomond area with a cast of 2,000. Disney's *Rob Roy: the Highland Rogue* (1954), with Richard Todd, another Irishman, shot on location, once more in the Aberfoyle area.

THE ROCKET POST (2002)

Camera crews can be a bit like buses – you wait ages and then a couple come together. First, the little Hebridean island of Taransay played host to *Castaway 2000*, the BBC's experiment of sticking an assorted mix of ordinary folk on an uninhabited island to see how they cope, then a film team arrived to shoot *The Rocket Post*. Its story was inspired by an experiment in the 1930s to use rockets to send mail between islands, but the film also focused on a romance between the German inventor and a local girl, against the growing international tension of the times. The film-makers chose Taransay only after failing to get permission to shoot on nearby Scarp, where the original demonstration took place. They also shot on Harris and Lewis, and at locations in the West Highlands.

DOUGRAY SCOTT

It was with envy and frustration that Dougray Scott looked at that famous *Trainspotting* poster and the rising careers of those pictured on it. He had been a regular on *Soldier, Soldier*, the hit television series that made Robson Green and Jerome Flynn household names, but it was because of his TV commitments that he missed the chance to star in one of the most important films ever made in Scotland. Strike one. Born Stephen Allan Scott, in St Andrews, Fife, he grew up in a poor part of Glenrothes. His father had various jobs, including selling fridges, though he had acted with the famous Unity Players in Glasgow. Scott studied drama at Kirkcaldy College of Technology, the same college as Ewan McGregor, though he was six years older. Scott surprised many when he quit *Soldier, Soldier* after just one series, but he was determined to break into films and time was not on his side. He appeared with Mickey Rourke in *Another 9½ Weeks*, but it failed to repeat the success of the original and went straight to video in the UK. A lead role as a corrupt cop in *Twin Town*, the new film from the producers of *Trainspotting*, should have set the ball rolling. It was supposed to do for Wales what *Trainspotting* had done for Scotland. It didn't. Strike two. He had been back in Scotland for a television adaptation of the Iain Banks novel *The Crow Road*, and for the small but memorable role of Robert Graves in *Regeneration*, another film that failed to fulfil box-office expectations. Then there was *Deep Impact*, a big-budget Hollywood disaster movie, in which he was Tea Leoni's boyfriend. It was a hit, but most of his scenes had been left on the cutting-room floor. Strike three. Then out of the blue came *Ever After*, a feminist reworking of *Cinderella* with Drew Barrymore as the feisty heroine. The makers were prepared to take a risk on an unknown as the prince, and so few people had seen Scott's previous films that he fitted the bill. He got the part after a screen test, researched the

Renaissance period, practised riding and fencing, and even claimed to draw inspiration from the story of Edward and Mrs Simpson. Between making *Ever After* and its release, Scott returned to Britain and made the partner-swapping drama *This Year's Love* and *Gregory's Two Girls*. Meanwhile, one of the few to see *Twin Town* was Tom Cruise, who decided the sullen Fifer would be perfect as Sean Ambrose, the megalomaniac renegade agent in *Mission: Impossible II*. Home run. He also landed the role of Wolverine, the most exciting of the *X-Men*, but unfortunately had to drop out because of delays on *MI2*. He returned to Britain (and once more to Scotland) to play the code-breaker hero of *Enigma*, an old-fashioned wartime thriller played out with a lot of flashbacks. The structure

Dougray Scott, picture courtesy of Peters, Fraser & Dunlop

75

afforded Scott the chance to romance both Kate Winslet and Saffron Burrows, whose disappearance sparks off his characters second career as an amateur detective. Scott had just the right anguished expression for the mathematical genius who cannot figure out why their relationship did not add up. He went on to star in *Cromwell and Fairfax*, as English civil war general Thomas Fairfax, with Tim Roth as Cromwell and Rupert Everett as Charles I, by which time he was finally in the major leagues along with the guys on the *Trainspotting* poster.

SHALLOW GRAVE (1994)

Andrew Macdonald and John Hodge were not exactly Hollywood high-flyers when they met at the Edinburgh International Film Festival in 1991. Macdonald was the grandson of Emeric Pressburger, one half of the Powell and Pressburger team that made such classics as *The Red Shoes*, but he was little more than a lowly production assistant who had directed a short film, *Dr Reitzer's Fragment*, in that year's programme. At least he was in the business. John Hodge was a junior hospital doctor who wanted to be a scriptwriter. Three years later they were back, having turned Hodge's scribbled plot outline into a feature film. *Shallow Grave* turned Macdonald, Hodge and director Danny Boyle, (the only non-Scot), into a force in British cinema and gave Ewan McGregor his big film break. It was a deliciously dark comedy-thriller, fast-moving and incredibly assured from the outset, as Boyle's camera takes the viewer on a rollercoaster ride through Edinburgh's fashionable and expensive New Town, over the cobbles of Heriot Row where Robert Louis Stevenson lived, along Great King Street and Drummond Place, down St Vincent Street to North East Circus Place, ostensibly the location of the flat in which much of the action takes place, though the actual stair is in nearby Scotland Street and the interior was built on the other side of the country in an empty warehouse in Glasgow. McGregor, Chris Eccleston and Kerry Fox play three affluent young professionals who rent out their spare room to a new flatmate, who promptly dies on them, leaving a suitcase of money behind. McGregor is a journalist and the film-makers shot in the Glasgow *Evening Times* offices in Albion Street; Fox is a doctor; Eccleston an accountant. The trio decide to keep the cash and dispose of the body, which they do at Rouken Glen on the outskirts of Glasgow, while the car was dumped at the flooded quarry at Mugdock Country Park, near Milngavie. The Scottish country dancing was shot at Glasgow's Townhouse Hotel in West George Street, which later closed down. The flatmates soon find themselves in violent conflict with the dead man's associates and each other. They manage to be attractive and amusing (or at least McGregor and Fox's characters do), and yet totally repugnant at the same time, and the film,

Christopher Eccleston, Kerry Fox and Ewan McGregor
in *Shallow Grave* (Channel Four Films)

made at the tail-end of Tory rule, captured the legacy of Thatcherism and the prevalent middle-class creed of always wanting more. 'This could have been any city,' Eccleston's disembodied voice declares in the opening voice-over. But it wasn't, it was Edinburgh. *Shallow Grave* helped to make Scotland fashionable as a location, proved it was possible for local talent to make films in Scotland and started a boom that would provide regular work for Scottish actors and crew. The makers took a chance on casting McGregor, an unknown 22-year-old, alongside Englishman Chris Eccleston and New Zealander Kerry Fox. Scotland had no young film stars at the time, but McGregor blazed a trail down which many other Scots would follow in the years ahead.

SHERLOCK HOLMES

Sir Arthur Conan Doyle's detective has appeared in more than 200 movies and has the distinction of being cinema's most filmed character. The author was born in Picardy Place, Edinburgh, and a statue of his most famous creation now stands near the site. Doyle acknowledged that the model for Holmes was not a detective, but Dr Joseph Bell, who taught medicine at Edinburgh University and was noted for his powers of observation and speedy diagnoses. Among those who have played Holmes are Basil Rathbone, Peter Cushing, Christopher Lee, George C. Scott, Roger Moore, Peter Cook and Christopher Plummer. Billy Wilder's *The Private Life of Sherlock Holmes* (1970) shot at Loch Ness.

SHORT FILMS

Twelve months before *Braveheart*'s triumph, Peter Capaldi, who played the gawky, young executive in *Local Hero*, won an Oscar for his film *Franz Kafka's It's a Wonderful Life*. A portrait of a writer struggling for inspiration, it drew on Kafka's surrealism, Capra's sentimentality and the black humour of the Glasgow streets and won the award for best live-action short in 1995. Scotland had already had some success in that Oscar category in 1981, with *The Dollar Bottom* which was based on a James Kennaway short story and was filmed in Edinburgh. It was, however, an 'incoming' production, made for Paramount. *Franz Kafka's It's a Wonderful Life* was one of the first Tartan Shorts, a scheme 'to promote emerging Scottish talent' organised by BBC Scotland and the Scottish Film Production Fund, one of the four organisations that joined together to form Scottish Screen.

Gasman by Lynne Ramsay

At much the same time, actor Peter Mullan made *Close* for £500. 'There was no great respect for short films,' he said, 'and then . . . suddenly everyone was running around with a 15-minute script.' Scottish Screen promoted several schemes, though Tartan Shorts remained the flagship, and subsequent films included Mullan's *Fridge* and Lynne Ramsay's *Gasman*, which brought Ramsay her second prize from the Cannes Film Festival, adding to one she got for her film school graduation film *Small Deaths*. Adrian McDowall won a BAFTA for *Who's My Favourite Girl?*, made as part of his Edinburgh College of Art course, while Jim Gillespie went to Hollywood on the back of *Joyride*, described as '*Die Hard* in the boot of a car', and directed *I Know What You Did Last Summer*.

STAR WARS

Ewan McGregor is not the only Scot who has made a significant contribution to *Star Wars*. His uncle, Denis Lawson, was fighter pilot Wedge in the original films; Ian McDiarmid, a distinguished stage actor from Carnoustie, was the duplicitous Palpatine in the originals and was still playing the part when McGregor joined the series; while Darth Maul was played by martial arts expert Ray Park, who is originally from Glasgow. Sebulba, the slimy creature in the *Phantom Menace* pod-race, was computer-generated but his voice belonged to Glasgow comic Lewis Macleod. Macleod might have wanted to keep quiet about it, but Sebulba's grotesque looks were based on Macleod's own features. David Brown was production supervisor on *The Phantom Menace*, and Trisha Biggar was costume designer on it and *Attack of the Clones*; both of whom were based in Glasgow. Some Scots have contributed without even knowing it. Ayrshire schoolboy James Robinson, who played the young William Wallace in *Braveheart*, was in line to play Anakin before a sudden growth spurt, but concept artist Iain McCaig did use him for early design sketches. McCaig, a Californian with Scottish ancestors, studied at Glasgow School of Art and was heavily influenced by Charles Rennie Mackintosh, the Glasgow designer and a leader of the Art Nouveau movement which employed flowing natural shapes. McCaig adopted Mackintosh's approach in designing Amidala's spectacular costumes and dubbed it Space Nouveau.

TILDA SWINTON

Once the darling of London's chattering classes, Tilda Swinton would do anything for her art – she stripped naked and slept with another woman in *Female Perversions*. And she prompted even more controversy when she kept her clothes on and slept by herself in London's Serpentine Gallery, a living, breathing, sleeping work of art. She was born Matilda Swinton in London on Guy Fawkes Day, 1960, but regards herself as a Scot. Daughter of the Lord-Lieutenant of Berwickshire, she went to Fettes College in Edinburgh and turned her back on London to live in Easter Ross with writer and artist John Byrne.

A slim redhead, with beautifully sculpted features and almost translucent skin, there is nevertheless a curiously androgynous, Bowie-esque quality about Swinton – in the play *Man to Man* she was a woman pretending to be a man; in the film *Orlando* her character begins as a man in Elizabethan times and ends up as a woman in the present; and in *Female Perversions* she was a high-powered lawyer, hiding her machismo behind lipstick and powder. Along the way Swinton appeared in *Your*

Tilda Swinton (photograph by David Gillanders)

Cheatin' Heart, which was written by Byrne, her fragile beauty was played down as the wife in *The War Zone*, and she was a regular in the arthouse films of Derek Jarman. After years of playing to the cultural elite, Swinton connected with a wider audience as the ruthless leader of the island commune in *The Beach* (2000) and was unlucky not to get at least an Oscar nomination for her performance in the thriller *The Deep End*, playing a mother covering up for her son after discovering his gay lover's corpse. *Young Adam* provided her with a starring role opposite Ewan McGregor and Peter Mullan.

TAGGART (1983–)

Taggart started as a one-off three-parter called *Killer*, with creator Glenn Chandler taking characters' names from Glasgow gravestones, but Mark McManus's sour-faced working-class Glasgow police detective proved so popular that Scottish Television continued to make mini-series and self-contained feature-length episodes even after McManus's death in 1994. Rather than replace him, they focused subsequently on his former colleagues – the rather stuffy Mike Jardine (James MacPherson) and the feisty Jackie Reid (Blythe Duff) – while still retaining the title *Taggart*. Eventually *Taggart* succeeded *Z Cars* as the longest-running police drama on British television. When Jardine was killed in 2002, the focus shifted again to DCI Matt Burke (Alex Norton). The show presented life, and death, in the raw and by 2002 had featured more than 200 deaths, from causes as varied as shooting and snakebite. At the height of its popularity it attracted a UK audience of more than 18 million and it has sold to more than 40 countries worldwide. *Taggart* filmed on location all over the Glasgow area and elsewhere, with the River Clyde figuring in numerous episodes, including the one in which Jardine meets his end.

THE 39 STEPS (1935, 1959, 1978)

An innocent man is suspected of murder, goes on the run and has to break a spy ring to prove his innocence – John Buchan's 1915 novel contains many elements that were to become staples of Alfred Hitchcock's oeuvre. He read the book not long after publication and decided he would like to turn it into a film, years before he directed his first movie. When he did get the chance to make the film, Hitchcock played fast and loose with Buchan's story, using only those elements which suited him. He moved the Scottish setting from Galloway to the Highlands, changed the 39 Steps from physical steps at the seaside to an organisation of spies, and introduced a romantic sub-plot – the scene in which Madeleine Carroll removes wet stockings while handcuffed to Robert Donat remains one of the sexiest ever. The mischievous director even insisted his stars stay handcuffed off-camera. Donat's character, Richard Hannay, makes his way north on the Flying Scotsman train after a mysterious woman is murdered in his London flat with a map of Scotland in her hand. With police closing in, Hannay dramatically escapes from the train on the Forth Bridge, a spectacular metal cantilever bridge, a mile and a half long and a marvel of Victorian engineering. The bridge is just outside Edinburgh, but on the far side Hannay finds himself not in Fife, but in the Highlands – geography not being Hitch's strongpoint. On a similar note, when it was pointed out that two different trains appear in quick succession during Hannay's journey, Hitch replied: 'There is something more important than logic; it is imagination.' The scene in which a woman's scream turns into the whistle of a train remains a landmark of early sound cinema. The film contains footage shot in Glen Coe, including the police pursuit, but all was not as it seemed. 'In the old days we always took artists on location. We rarely do that today. The scenes where Madeleine and Robert were going through the Highlands were all made with "doubles",' Hitch told the *News Chronicle* back in 1937. '"No," you will say. "I saw them talking in close-ups during the Highland sequences." But there's an answer to that: a pair of scissors. You take the first shot of the moorland with the two figures running across it – these are the doubles. Then you cut to a close-up which you have taken in the studio.' The film shot mainly in London's Lime Grove Studios, where sheep disrupted production by eating the carefully arranged heather and bracken. A lacklustre 1959 colour remake, with Kenneth More, followed Hitch's film almost shot for shot, filming at the Forth Bridge and Dunblane, Killin and elsewhere in Perthshire. The third version, starring Robert Powell, stuck more closely to Buchan's novel and returned the action to the south-west of Scotland, where locations included Castlemilk House near Lockerbie, Morton Castle near Thornhill, the village of Durisdeer, the Forest of Ae and Drumlanrig estate, although the bridge was the Victoria Bridge on the Severn Valley Railway.

TRAINSPOTTING (1996)

It was hailed by *Empire* and *Time Out* as the best British film of the decade. While *Braveheart* came, saw, conquered and scurried off back to Hollywood, *Trainspotting* was made by Scots, with Scots in virtually all the leading roles. It launched or boosted a couple of dozen film careers, in front of and behind the cameras – careers which have lasted longer than many of the locations on which the film shot. Rouken Glen, on the outskirts of Glasgow, where Ewan McGregor and Jonny Lee Miller shoot the skinhead's dog, and Rannoch Moor, the destination for the abortive trip to the countryside, are both still there of course. So are Princes Street and Calton Road, in Edinburgh city centre, where Ewan McGregor and Ewen Bremner are pursued by store detectives at the beginning of the film. But, although it is set in Edinburgh, most of the filming was in Glasgow, and many of the locations have closed or been demolished, testimony to the changing character of the city.

Irvine Welsh's novel *Trainspotting* was published in 1993, the year *Shallow Grave* was made. Welsh's stories of Edinburgh low-life were real and immediate, straight off the schemes. Many episodes, such as the one in which a character covers everyone with crap, seemed designed to disgust readers, but are deceptively well crafted and genuinely funny. Welsh substituted a delight in the absurd in place of the anger of the social-realist school of working-class drama and connected with a large and youthful audience. John Hodge's adaptation concentrated on Mark Renton (McGregor), though there was still room for an unusually strong supporting cast of chancers, losers and misfits. Ewen Bremner, who played the hapless Spud, had played Renton in a stage version, but Kelly Macdonald was a newcomer, hired as a result of open auditions, and Kevin McKidd was recruited on the strength of the rushes from *Small Faces*. Robert Carlyle was brilliant as the

Ewan McGregor in *Trainspotting* (Figment / Channel Four Films)

psychopathic Francis Begbie. The only non-Scot in a major role was Jonny Lee Miller, who, ironically, got the part of Sick Boy because of the quality of his Sean Connery impression, but then his grandfather, Bernard Lee, had played M.

Sets were constructed in the old Wills' cigarette factory in Alexandra Parade, Glasgow, which was subsequently redeveloped as offices, and in the George Hotel, Buchanan Street, which was demolished though the facade was retained as part of the Virgin megastore. The football sequence at the beginning was shot at the Firhill complex in Hopehill Road. Renton and Spud share a milkshake in Jaconelli's café in Maryhill Road, before Spud's hilarious job interview on speed at the Whiteinch baths (now closed). Renton meets Diane (Macdonald) at the Volcano disco in Benalder Street, another location that has disappeared. The old folks' home, from which Renton and Spud remove the TV, was at Canniesburn Hospital, a regular spot for film and television producers, though that part was later converted to flats. The bar in which the American tourist is mugged was the London Road Tavern, beside Celtic Park; the bar in which Begbie starts a fight was Crosslands in Queen Margaret Drive, and the one in which he plays pool was the old Wills' social club. The exterior of Tommy's flat was in Nitshill and Darnley, and the exterior of Swanney's flat was in Govan – it was later demolished, which seems par for the course. The station on Rannoch Moor is Corrour, and Renton and his friends get the bus to London from the Buchanan Street bus station.

If *Braveheart* gave Scotland a belief in itself, *Trainspotting* made the country positively cool. Welsh's portrait of junkie Edinburgh might have made for a heavy, depressing movie, but writer John Hodge and director Danny Boyle presented real – and for the most part undesirable – characters with more than a dash of surrealism and a huge amount of style, humour and energy, leaving the viewer almost breathless.

2001: A SPACE ODYSSEY (1968)

Mostly locations appear as themselves, but occasionally they are used as an unnamed backdrop or to double for somewhere else entirely. Glasgow City Chambers stood in for the Vatican in the film *Heavenly Pursuits* and the tiny picturesque village of Port Logan in South West of Scotland made a very convincing island in the television series *2000 Acres of Sky*. Stanley Kubrick may have been the ultimate perfectionist, but there was never any question of him filming on location on Jupiter when he made *2001: A Space Odyssey*, his epic exploration of space, the human condition and the meaning of life in the hippy-dippy '60s. It shot mainly in the studios at Shepperton and Borehamwood, near London, but Scotland figured in the sequence in which spaceman David Bowman (Keir Dullea) speeds towards Jupiter, over a fleeting world of ever-changing texture and colour. Kubrick combined aerial footage of the desert landscape of Monument Valley in the United States, a recurring location in the John Ford Westerns, and of the peat bogs and mountains of the Outer Hebrides, using colour filters to produce a suitably psychedelic trip. The bare ancient rocks on the east coast of Harris look especially other-worldly and were just what Kubrick wanted.

WHISKY GALORE! (1949)

It was not through any great artistic vision that first-time director Sandy Mackendrick chose to shoot *Whisky Galore!* 500 miles from London, on location in the Outer Hebrides where the events that inspired Compton Mackenzie's comic novel took place. It was simply that Ealing Studios were full and the company was desperate for films to counter a dearth of Hollywood movies. So, in 1948 a cast and crew of 80 descended on the peaceful little island of Barra, a six-hour ferry journey from Oban. They stayed in the homes of the islanders, had to contend with the worst summer weather for 80 years, and went over budget and over schedule. Mackenzie's story of a ship that runs aground carrying 50,000 cases of whisky, and the islanders' attempts to salvage it, was inspired by the wreck of the SS *Politician* off Eriskay in 1941 and similar attempts to retrieve its liquid cargo. It was a popular joke that it was the first time a politician had ever done anyone any good. Mackenzie lived on Barra, though the island was renamed in the book and film, as Todday, after the term for a hot alcoholic drink, and the *Politician* became the *Cabinet Minister*. Mackendrick shot all over Barra, and many locations remain readily recognisable. The village of Castlebay has changed little; Kisimul Castle still sits on its islet a stone's throw from the shore; the church, Our Lady, Star of the Sea, whose clock signalled the start of the sabbath and a delay in salvage operations, is still there; the bank is still a bank, albeit now the Royal Bank of Scotland rather than the Commercial Bank of Scotland. The old post office served as the island store and the schoolhouse at Borve was Gordon Jackson's schoolhouse in the film. More recently it has been used as emergency accommodation for the homeless. The old Castlebay police house, where council offices stand today, was home to English Home Guard captain Waggett (Basil Radford). Beach scenes were shot at Allasdale, Eoligarry and on the neighbouring island of Vatersay, now linked to Barra by causeway. *Whisky Galore!* was not a hit when it first appeared, and although it has become one of the most popular of Ealing comedies, critics have sometimes dismissed it as stereotypical and patronising. What has ensured its continuing popularity is its dry subversive humour, and its authentic sense of place. 'A happy people with few and simple pleasures,' says the opening voice-over, as nine children appear, one after the other, through a croft-house door. Several men who took whisky from the SS *Politician* were convicted and sent to jail, whereas in the film a criminal Celtic brotherhood outwits the English authority figure. This was no auteur effort: as a presbyterian, with a strong work ethic, Mackendrick saw Waggett as the hero and wanted to make him a kilted Scottish laird. It was producer Monja Danischewsky, a Russian Jew, who promoted the romantic vision of a remote community fighting foreign interference, reflected in the punning American title *Tight Little Island*. By all accounts the film was a mess and another Ealing director, Charles Crichton, was brought in at the editing stage. A sequel, *Rockets Galore!*, also shot on Barra.

THE WICKER MAN (1974)

The major cinema chains simply did not want *The Wicker Man* when it was completed in 1973 and a cut-down version finally went out the following year as the bottom half of a double bill. Yet today it has a cult following and figures in lists of the best British films ever. The cult was fuelled by urban myths – Rod Stewart wanting to buy the negative and destroy it, so no one would see his girlfriend Britt Ekland's backside, though she had a botty double in the film anyway; rumours of lost footage buried in the foundations of the M3, though three different versions of

The Wicker Man

© Bartholomew Ltd 2002

the film, including the original director's cut, survive. The other reason *The Wicker Man* has acquired such a cult following, and why it is now so highly rated, is the quality and unique nature of the film itself. Edward Woodward plays police sergeant Howie, who flies to the remote island of Summerisle to investigate a report of a missing child. He is seen flying over Skye and the rock known as the Old Man of Storr (1), before arriving in the sheltered bay at Plockton (2), a village in Wester Ross that was home to Hamish Macbeth. It is on the Gulf Stream and the sight of palm trees affords an early hint of the strangeness of the film and the importance of nature in the plot. There is a group of islands called the Summer Isles in Wester Ross, but the film's Summerisle was a combination of mainland locations, mainly in the south-west of Scotland. Director Robin Hardy used the colourfully painted houses and the little closes of Kirkcudbright (3) for the village. It also supplied the mainland police station. The Cally Estate offices in Gatehouse of Fleet (4) served as the Green Man Inn, where Willow (Ekland), the landlord's daughter, attempts to seduce Howie, though the bar scenes were shot in the Ellangowan Hotel in Creetown (5). Willow's bedroom was at the Cally offices, while Howie's room, which is supposedly an adjoining room, was in a private house in Whithorn (6). The shops in the film were dotted around, in Kirkcudbright, Gatehouse and Creetown, and the library was the library in Whithorn. Lord Summerisle (Christopher Lee) lives in Culzean Castle (7) in Ayrshire, a rather grand property for such a remote little island. The viewer is

The Wicker Man (British Lion)

never entirely sure how big Summerisle is meant to be – it has its own registrar, but no resident policeman, but that just adds a slightly disorientating edge to events. The grounds of Summerisle's castle were a combination of Logan Botanic Garden (8) and Castle Kennedy Gardens (9), near Stranraer. It is in the latter that girls are seen dancing naked. Lochinch Castle (10), at one end of Castle Kennedy Gardens, was used for some interiors of Summerisle's castle. At the island school Howie finds boys dancing round a maypole, while teacher Diane Cilento explains its symbolism to the girls. Howie suspects the missing girl has been the victim of human sacrifice and is buried in the churchyard. Hardy used the old schoolhouse, now a holiday cottage, and the churchyard and roofless church at Anwoth (11), a peaceful hamlet up a country lane off the A75 between Gatehouse and Creetown. Everything falls into place for the film's shock ending, when a human sacrifice must be burned inside a giant wicker man, a sequence filmed on the promontory at Burrow Head (12) and nearby St Ninian's Cave, on the south-eastern tip of Wigtownshire. What is truly chilling about *The Wicker Man* is not simply that the residents of Summerisle burn people, but that they keep bursting into jolly songs about the cycle of life, like mad refugees from a second-rate musical. Summerisle is located somewhere between reality and fantasy and the film treads a narrow line between greatness and camp folly, but because everyone treats it seriously, it works brilliantly.

WRITERS

The Scot who has contributed most to cinema might arguably be neither an actor nor a director, but novelist Robert Louis Stevenson. There have been about 100 films directly based on his novels and stories. Robert Newton, Orson Welles, Charlton Heston and even the Muppets have had a go at *Treasure Island*, though *Dr Jekyll and Mr Hyde* has proved even more popular and incredibly adaptable. Stevenson was born at 8 Howard Place, Edinburgh, and died in Samoa in 1894. His tale of a scientific experiment and split personality – one half good, the other evil – was first filmed just 14 years later and Frederic March won an Oscar for his performance in the 1931 version. The story got a gender-bending twist in Hammer's *Dr Jekyll and Sister Hyde* and the 1995 comedy *Dr Jekyll and Ms Hyde*; there was a Tom and Jerry version and *Mary Reilly* retold the story from Jekyll's maid's perspective. *The Black Arrow*, *The Body Snatcher*, *The Bottle Imp*, *The Ebb-Tide*, *Kidnapped*, *The Master of Ballantrae*, *The Suicide Club* and *St Ives* have all been filmed more than once.

Sir Arthur Conan Doyle and J.M. Barrie made a major contribution to cinema with Sherlock Holmes and Peter Pan, and J.K. Rowling, although English, was resident in Edinburgh when she set Harry Potter's adventures on paper. All three characters have their own entries elsewhere in this book. Dozens of Scottish novelists have had books filmed, from Sir Walter Scott, the author of *Rob Roy* and *Ivanhoe*, through John Buchan, whose ripping yarn *The 39 Steps* has been filmed three times, and Muriel Spark, who wrote *The Prime of Miss Jean Brodie*. One novelist worth a special mention is Alistair MacLean, whose novels sold in enormous numbers in the '60s, '70s and '80s and who provided storylines for a string of big-budget Hollywood and British action movies, beginning with *The Guns of Navrone* (1961), and including *Ice Station Zebra*, *Where Eagles Dare* and *When Eight Bells Toll*, which shot on Mull and Staffa.

Neil Paterson was in his time a journalist, Dundee United footballer and novelist. His script for *The Kidnappers* (1953) was based on one of his own stories, but it was for his adaptation of John Braine's novel *Room at the Top* that he won an Oscar in 1960. James Kennaway was nominated in the same category the following year for the adaptation of his own novel *Tunes of Glory*. George MacDonald Fraser created a new series of adventures for *Flashman*, the bully from *Tom Brown's Schooldays*, and scripted the 1973 version of *The Three Musketeers* and *Octopussy*. Allan Shiach managed to combine running his family's Macallan whisky business with a career as a script-writer, under the name Allan Scott, and his credits include the adaptations of *Don't Look Now* and *The Witches*.

One of Scotland's most remarkable film writers is Alan Sharp, the Clydeside shipyard worker, whose novel *A Green Tree in Gedde* brought him enormous acclaim in 1965. He went to Hollywood after his second book and had five scripts filmed in quick succession – the Peter Fonda western *The Hired Hand*; the thriller *The Last Run*; *Ulzana's Raid*, one of the truly great 1970s westerns; *Billy Two Hats*, yet another western, with Gregory Peck as an expat Scot; and *Night Moves*, with Gene Hackman as a small-time private detective. It is a remarkable body of Americana for someone from Greenock. But Scott drifted into the obscurity of American television before producer Peter Broughan persuaded him to write *Rob Roy*.

John Hodge, a doctor by profession, made his mark with *Shallow Grave* and won an Oscar nomination for his adaption of *Trainspotting*, and Paul Laverty, a former lawyer, has written a series of screenplays set in Scotland for director Ken Loach including *My Name is Joe* and *Sweet Sixteen*. Other contemporary Scottish writers breaking into film include Irvine Welsh (*Trainspotting*, *The Acid House*), Alan Warner whose novel *Morvern Caller* was adapted for director Lynne Ramsey's second feature, and Iain Banks whose book *The Crow Road* became a popular television drama, and whose novel *Complicity* was made into a feature film.

YOUNG ADAM (2002)

Seven years after *Trainspotting*, Ewan McGregor returned to Scotland as the conquering hero to star in *Young Adam*, along with Tilda Swinton, the most exciting Scottish actress of her generation. The film also marked a reunion with Peter Mullan, who had supplied McGregor with drugs in *Trainspotting* and broken into his flat in *Shallow Grave*. Alexander Trocchi's dark, erotic source novel had acquired a cult reputation since it first appeared almost half a century earlier. McGregor is Joe, a drifter who is given a job by barge-owner Les (Mullan). One day they find the corpse of a young woman in the water and, as police investigate, it becomes increasingly clear Joe knows more than he is admitting. Meanwhile, he becomes involved with Les's wife, played by Swinton. 'This could be the first ever genuinely erotic, sexy Scottish film,' Mullan predicted while on location on the Forth and Clyde Canal. The film shot at various points on the Forth and Clyde Canal and the Union Canal, including Linlithgow and Bowling. Other locations included Glasgow, Grangemouth Docks, Paisley and Perth. It was a difficult shoot and Mullan was incapacitated with a back injury at one point, but expectations remained as high as for any movie made in Scotland over the last few years. The film was directed by David Mackenzie, brother of *Monarch of the Glen* star Alastair Mackenzie.

Tilda Swinton in *Young Adam* (Recorded Picture Company / Sigma)

Quick Reference

Sponsors

Scottish Screen

Scottish Screen is working to establish Scotland as an important European screen production centre while projecting Scotland's culture to the world. As  the national body responsible for developing every aspect of film, television and broadcast new media, it allocates National Lottery funds to develop feature scripts and invests in feature production. Through short-film schemes such as Tartan Shorts, New Found Lands, Cineworks and 8½, it provides opportunities for film-makers at all stages of their careers. Scottish Screen also supports local film theatres; finds and preserves historical footage and maintains the national film archive; provides a wide range of training and development opportunities for the industry including the highly regarded New Entrants Training course; and operates a locations service which provides expert advice to attract productions from the UK and overseas.

The Scottish Highlands and Islands Film Commission

A film liaison service has been operated by the Highland Council since 1993. In 1997 a partnership was formed with five other local authorities in the north of Scotland, creating a  film commission which covers almost a third of Scotland. The Scottish Highlands and Islands Commission looks after the Shetland Islands, Orkney Islands, Western Isles, Moray, and Argyll and Bute – locations from Lerwick to Campbeltown – providing free advice and information for production crews, access to a digital locations library, an on-line production guide of local cast, crew and facilities, and support for recces.

The British Council

The British Council presents the contemporary face of the UK through the arts, and nurtures cultural and creative dialogue between nations. Many of its projects involve UK artists collaborating with overseas contemporaries, with results that are exciting both for the arts world and international understanding. The main purpose of the Film and Television Department is to expand international audiences for new work from Britain. Film festivals are an extremely effective way of enabling large numbers of predominantly young people to regularly refresh their perceptions of the UK.

VisitScotland

VisitScotland acts as a marketing body to attract visitors to Scotland from the UK and overseas. It leads the industry and provides strategic guidance to help increase visitor expenditure by developing the seasonal and geographical spread of tourism. It advises the industry and the Scottish Executive on ways to improve the variety, value and quality of product across an extremely diverse range. Film tourism is playing an increasing role in Scotland's ability to market itself and it is an area which VisitScotland is keen to develop for both the domestic and overseas markets, making Scotland a must-visit destination.